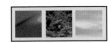

Geography of Extreme Environments

DESERTS

POLAR REGIONS

THE TROPICS

Extreme Climates

Desert

Ice Covered

Tundra

Wet tropics

Polar Regions

Charles F. Gritzner
South Dakota State University

CHELSEA HOUSE
PUBLISHERS
An imprint of Infobase Publishing

This book is dedicated with deepest gratitude to H. Jesse Walker,
Louisiana State University Boyd Professor Emeritus, for his half-century of friendship,
encouragement, and support that opened the author's eyes to the importance of geographic
education and to the fascinating natural environment and cultures of the Arctic.

FRONTIS The Polar Regions, Wet Tropics, and Deserts are highlighted on this map of the world's extreme climates.

Polar Regions

Chelsea House
An imprint of Infobase Publishing
132 West 31st Street
New York, NY 10001

Library of Congress Cataloging-in-Publication Data

Gritzner, Charles F.
  Polar regions / Charles F. Gritzner.
    p. cm. — (Geography of extreme environments)
  Includes bibliographical references and index.
  ISBN 0-7910-9235-6 (hardcover)
1. Polar regions—Description and travel—Juvenile literature. I. Title.
  G587.G75 2006
  910.911—dc22

Chelsea House books are available at special discounts when purchased in bulk quantities for businesses, associations, institutions, or sales promotions. Please call our Special Sales Department in New York at (212) 967-8800 or (800) 322-8755.

You can find Chelsea House on the World Wide Web at http://www.chelseahouse.com

Series design by Keith Trego
Cover design by Ben Peterson

Printed in the United States of America

Bang KT 10 9 8 7 6 5 4 3 2 1

This book is printed on acid-free paper.

All links and Web addresses were checked and verified to be correct at the time of publication. Because of the dynamic nature of the Web, some addresses and links may have changed since publication and may no longer be valid.

1 Introducing the Polar World   **7**

2 Weather and Climate   **16**

3 Snow, Ice, and Frozen Ground   **34**

4 Landforms and Ecosystems   **46**

5 Native Peoples   **62**

6 European Influences   **76**

7 Contemporary Conditions and Regions   **93**

8 Future Prospects for the Polar World   **109**

Historical Geography at a Glance   **114**

Bibliography   **117**

Further Reading   **118**

Index   **121**

Introducing
the Polar World

Welcome to Earth's last great frontier—the Polar World! Here, in the "land of the midnight sun," the human imprint is dwarfed by nature's harshness. Located at the "ends of the earth," the polar environment is one dominated by bone-chilling cold. Low temperature, more than any other factor, is the agent primarily affecting the region's natural landscapes and patterns of human adaptation. Cold shapes the patterned land, freezes the waters, and creates and preserves glacial ice. Both plant and animal life must be uniquely adapted to cold in order to survive the seemingly endless polar winters. Lakes and streams, too, show the influence of past and present frigid conditions.

Nature presents equally difficult and often unforgiving obstacles for humans to overcome if they are to survive in the Polar World. For thousands of years, though, people have inhabited the Arctic region. Some hardy peoples, such as North America's Inuit (Eskimo),

Three Inuit girls play a traditional game during the celebration of the establishment of Canada's newest province, Nunavut, on March 31, 1999. Inuit people have adapted well to the Arctic's harsh environment by utilizing the resources around them. For example, caribou hides provide warmth and protection from the elements in the winter.

learned long ago how to survive—and actually thrive—in this harsh and seemingly inhospitable environment.

LOCATING THE POLAR WORLD

Strangely, there is little agreement in regard to the name, definition, or even location of the Polar World. Some writers refer to the region simply as "the north." Others prefer "the Arctic." Since poles and extreme conditions exist in both hemispheres, the term *polar* (world, region, realm, or environment) is generally used for both areas. The southern continent of Antarctica will receive little attention in this book, however, because it has no native or permanent population and has no economic significance.

Geographers and others also have identified numerous factors by which the Polar World can be defined. First and foremost, a region is defined as an area possessing one or more homogeneous, or uniform, elements. In the Polar World, of course, the primary element is temperature, but there are many others. The following descriptions, limited to the Northern Hemisphere, are often used to define the region. None of them, alone, is completely satisfactory.

- **The Polar World is located poleward of the Arctic Circle.** Perhaps the most commonly used criterion is the Arctic Circle, that imaginary line surrounding the globe at 66 1/2 degrees north latitude. The line marks the point at which on at least one day a year the sun will not rise and another on which it will not set. Within this area, however, temperatures and other conditions vary greatly.
- **The Polar World is in the "Frigid Zone."** Early Greek geographers divided Earth into three zones: torrid, temperate, and frigid. The border between the temperate and frigid zones is generally placed at 60 degrees north and south latitude. As you shall see, however, latitude, itself, is a very unreliable determinant of climatic conditions.
- **The average temperature of the warmest month in the Polar World falls below 50°F (10°C).** Severity of temperature becomes a major environmental factor when the average temperature of the warmest month falls below 50°F. Vegetation is sparse, water remains in frozen form much of the year, and other difficult conditions occur. Temperature alone, however, is inadequate in defining the region: Extreme cold also occurs at high elevation in the equatorial zone and elsewhere.
- **The Polar World contains permafrost.** Where winters are long and frigid and summers are short and cool, ground beneath the surface remains permanently frozen.

Nearly all of the Polar World is underlain by this condition called permafrost. Permafrost, however, extends far south of the region's normal limits, particularly at higher elevations.

- **The Polar World is above the treeline.** As you may have seen on high mountains, there is an upward limit to tree growth called the "treeline." This zone, created by low temperatures in which trees can no longer survive, also occurs at higher latitudes. It generally coincides with areas

Using a Compass in the Polar World

Does your compass always point to true north or to the North Pole? Well, that depends! If you stood at the North Pole with a magnetic compass, it would point south! The North Pole, of course, is located at 90 degrees north latitude, or "true north." A compass needle, however, will point to magnetic north, a location that is constantly changing. Currently, it is located at near 83 degrees north latitude and 114 degrees west longitude. To complicate things, it is also moving toward Siberia at a rate of about 25 miles (40 kilometers) per year.

What does this mean with regard to your compass arrow? The answer to that question depends on your location. If you were in Biloxi, Mississippi, in 2005, your compass would point to both magnetic and true north. You would be on what is called the agonic line, a roughly north-south line along which there is no magnetic error. If, on the other hand, you were in Fairbanks, Alaska, in 2005, your compass would point 22 degrees 47 minutes east of true north—quite an error if you are lost in the taiga! The following Canadian Web site can be used to determine the precise declination for any location on Earth's surface: *http://gsc.nrcan.gc.ca/geomag/apps/mdcal_e .php.*

in which the warmest monthly temperature falls below 50°F (10°C).

All these factors contribute to the uniqueness of the Polar World, yet none of them by itself completely defines the region. If considered alone, most would include midlatitude and even tropical locations, where frigid conditions occur at high elevations. Straight lines, such as the boundary between the Greek-defined temperate and frigid zones or the Arctic Circle

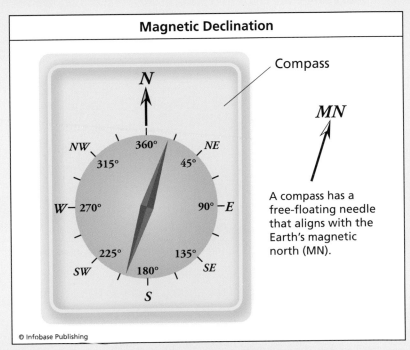

Magnetic Declination

Compass

MN

A compass has a free-floating needle that aligns with the Earth's magnetic north (MN).

© Infobase Publishing

Magnetic declination is defined as the difference between true north (the axis around which the earth rotates) and magnetic north (the direction the needle of a compass will point). The closer one is to the poles, the larger the variance in compass readings.

(66 1/2 degrees north latitude) are inadequate determiners. Too many factors contribute to temperatures and the environmental conditions they create. Physical criteria also ignore people and the ways they have learned to live successfully in this harsh, remote, and often merciless region. For purposes of this book, the Polar World is defined in the following terms:

- **Living in the Polar World involves cultural adaptation to severe conditions.** It is that part of the world in which peoples' way of life must be adapted to severe cold and other natural conditions, such as the duration of sunlight and darkness and frozen ground, that occur within the polar environment.

  Cultural ecology—how people culturally adapt to, use, and change the lands in which they live—has long been a major focus of geographic research. Understanding these relationships is one of the geographer's most important tasks. Thus defined, most of the Polar World lies north of 60 degrees north latitude, although there are exceptions. It includes all lands surrounding the Arctic Ocean. Politically, much of Alaska, northern Canada, and all of Greenland lie within the Polar World, as do portions of Norway, Sweden, Finland, and all of northern Russia. (Iceland lies physically within the region but is excluded, because its population and culture are European.)

  Through time, the Polar World has expanded and contracted. During the ice age, in some places, it extended southward by several thousand miles. Huge ice sheets reached as far south in the United States as the present-day Ohio and Missouri rivers. Today, the Polar World is shrinking. Evidence suggests that our planet is warming, particularly in the Arctic region. If this trend continues, the Polar World will continue to shrink in size.

Most people think of the polar region as the world's most remote location. In reality, though, it is the "hub" of the world.

Ninety degrees north latitude, or the North Pole, occupies the center of the Northern Hemisphere. As can easily be seen on a globe, about 70 percent of the world's land area lies north of the equator. In addition, more than three-fourths of the world's population is clustered in the Northern Hemisphere. As you will learn elsewhere in this book, the polar region plays a very important role in military strategy, intercontinental air travel, and even trade and commerce.

MIDLATITUDE PEOPLES LOOK NORTHWARD

To midlatitude peoples, the Polar World has long been considered a remote and alien land. The earliest documented exploration of the Polar Region by Mediterranean Europeans did not take place until the fourth century B.C. More than a thousand years ago, Viking voyagers ventured westward across the North Atlantic, reaching Iceland, Greenland, and eventually North America. Following Columbus's voyages, Europeans began to seek a water route to the riches of the Orient. The search drew explorers into the Arctic Ocean, where they sought a route across the "top" of North America and Eurasia (Europe and Asia). Gradually, other explorers began to provide details that helped fill in the many blank spots on maps of the Arctic region. Some were simply adventurers; others came to seek their fortune in gold or the valuable pelts of fur-bearing animals. Still others came as missionaries, scientists, and government administrators.

Only recently has the region begun to attract permanent settlers from the warmer midlatitudes in growing numbers. Some are rugged "loners," people with a pioneering spirit who are attracted by the region's many challenges and the seclusion offered by its isolation. Most, however, are drawn by the Polar World's rich storehouse of natural resources. Economic development, political integration, and population growth have brought about many changes within the region. Throughout most of the Polar World, however, the impact of

Due to its frigid climate, the Polar Region is sparsely inhabited. Throughout much of its history, the region has largely been inhabited by only Natives and adventure seekers. Because communities—such as the one pictured here in Alaska—are so isolated, oftentimes the only way to travel is by floatplane.

outside influences is relatively recent. Alaska did not become a U.S. territory until 1912 and a state until 1959, and the oil boom that doubled its population and sent its economy soaring did not get under way until the late 1970s. Today, visitors to Anchorage, Fairbanks, or other major Alaskan urban centers would feel as "at home" there as they would in the lower 48 U.S. states.

A LAND OF PROSPECTS AND PROBLEMS

Most readers, no doubt, are aware of the huge controversy surrounding the rich petroleum and natural gas deposits located in the Arctic National Wildlife Refuge (ANWR). In essence, the issue is whether to develop an essential natural resource, or is it more important to preserve a pristine natural landscape and its wildlife? It is a conflict being played out with various themes, scales, and consequences throughout much of the Polar World. Midlatitude peoples and needs are often in sharp conflict with local populations, values, and environments. In addition, the intrusion of foreign peoples and cultures has often resulted in abrupt and often painful shocks to native peoples and their traditional culture (way of life).

The polar environment is also being severely threatened. During the last century, the Soviet Union dumped military waste, including highly toxic nuclear material, into the Arctic Ocean. Many fishing grounds, such as Canada's Grand Banks, are becoming severely depleted. The huge and majestic blue whales of northern waters have been hunted to near extinction. Caribou herds are declining in number throughout northern America. The greatest threat, however, may come from nature itself. Warming temperatures during recent decades have introduced what could be devastating changes throughout much of the Arctic region. This may sound strange to those who live in the midlatitudes, but you must remember: The Polar World is a region defined by and well adapted to the cold.

In this book, you will learn about the basic geographic conditions and patterns of the Polar World. Our investigation begins with the region's atmospheric conditions, because weather and climate dominate all other elements of the environment. You will learn about native peoples and how they have ingeniously adapted to the region's harsh natural conditions. We will then follow the early European explorers as they ventured into the Arctic's "northern mists." Our trip through the Polar World would not be complete without visiting present-day peoples and the places in which they live. You will have an opportunity to learn about their social, economic, political, and other important cultural activities. Finally, we will gaze into a geographical crystal ball and attempt to get a glimpse of the region's future. Put on your warmest clothing, and let us head northward to begin our journey to and through the extreme environment of the Polar World!

2

Weather
and Climate

Nothing defines the Polar World better than its weather and climate. Cold, in particular, is the primary control affecting all other elements of the natural environment. It is also the chief condition to which humans must adapt if they are to survive in the region. On a day-by-day basis, weather is constantly changing. Over periods of time measured by decades and longer, climate remains quite constant. As you will learn in this chapter, the region is dominated by severe cold, but it also offers occasional surprises.

CLIMATE

Climate is defined as the long-term average condition of the weather in a particular area; hence, it is somewhat easier to understand and explain than weather. When considering the Polar World, we normally think in very general terms. Perhaps the descriptions "severe cold," "lots of snow and ice," and "howling winds" come to mind. These are average conditions that hold true over long periods of time and throughout most of the region. By our standards, the Arctic is often described with such words as *cold, bleak, barren,* and *monotonous.*

Many factors must be taken into consideration when defining and classifying atmospheric conditions by climate type. In this book, we will identify three climatic realms into which all or part of the Polar World falls. It should be noted, however, that many climatic classifications exist; they are based on a variety of arbitrarily selected criteria and are identified by many names.

Polar Ice Cap

The coldest climatic region is the polar ice cap—those areas where land lies deeply buried beneath glacial ice. Here, frost is perpetual, and all months have an average temperature below 32°F (0°C). Moisture is scant. This region, believe it or not, is often called a "polar desert," because it receives only a few inches of precipitation each year. During the ice ages of the Pleistocene era (1.8 million to 10,000 years ago), this climate expanded far southward, even into the northern interior of the United States. Today, the island of Greenland and the continent of Antarctica are the only locations where this climate occurs. Ice caps are uninhabited, except for a small number of scientists and government employees.

Subpolar

This region is also called the *tundra,* named for its scant vegetation. The subpolar climate is defined as areas in which at least one month has an average temperature above 32°F (0°C) but below 50°F (10°C). Winters are very long and harsh, and summers are extremely short. It is often said, perhaps only half jokingly, that "It is always winter up here, but July is bad for sledding and skiing!" Here, too, annual precipitation is sparse, amounting to less than 10 inches (25 centimeters) in most locations. This is the climate of the islands within the Arctic Ocean and those lands occupying the northernmost fringe

The taiga is a subarctic forest largely made up of needleleaf coniferous trees. Much of Alaska, central and northern Canada, interior northern Eurasia, and Russian Siberia fall within this region. Pictured here is an aerial view of the Siberian taiga in Russia.

of North America and Eurasia. Although the region has been home to native cultures for thousands of years, today's population remains very sparse and widely scattered. Midlatitude peoples have only begun to settle within the region, drawn by the prospect of wealth from the area's resources.

Subarctic

This area is also called the *taiga*, named for the vast boreal forest that spreads across most of the region and its "humid-continental short summer." Here, the coldest month is below freezing, but the warmest month is above 50°F (10°C). Winters are long and cold, but summer lasts several months, and temperatures can get surprisingly high. Precipitation varies greatly, with most locations receiving between 10 and 30 inches

(25 and 75 centimeters). The subarctic covers much of Alaska, central and northern Canada, and much of interior northern Eurasia, including most of Russian Siberia. Population is generally low and widely scattered. In both North America and Eurasia, some urbanization has occurred based on administrative functions or local economic development.

MYTHS AND MISCONCEPTIONS

As is true of all extreme environments, Polar World climates conjure up many myths and misconceptions. Before considering the specific controls and conditions, let's discuss some of the more widely held beliefs.

Cold, Frozen Wasteland

Only the interior of Greenland and most of Antarctica can correctly be described as a cold, frozen wasteland. As you will soon learn, the Polar World has actually recorded higher temperatures than most tropical locations. In fact, many midlatitude locations experience both lower winter extremes and lower winter average temperatures than do a number of locations in the Arctic. The author lives in Brookings, South Dakota (44 degrees north latitude), and for many years, he traveled to Alaska in January or February to conduct workshops for teachers. During about 20 such trips, only once was it colder in Anchorage (or several other Alaskan communities) than it was in South Dakota!

Vast Quantities of Snow

The polar region, you will remember, is a "desert," receiving fewer than 10 inches (25 centimeters) of precipitation annually, most of which falls as summer rain. Low amounts of precipitation and high winds actually keep the Arctic surface (particularly the subpolar climate) snow-free during much of the winter. It is a popular myth that the Inuit (Eskimo) built snow igloos because there is so much snow. Nothing could be further from the truth. If the availability of snow determined the type of building material used, native peoples in California's Sierra Nevada, where some places receive up to 700 inches (1,778 centimeters) of snowfall each winter, would be building igloos! Roughly one-half of the United States receives more snow each winter than does anyplace in the Polar World.

Glacial Ice

One popular myth is that glacial ice is found only in polar regions. Glacial ice forms in those locations where snowfall accumulation exceeds loss through evaporation and melting. These conditions, resulting in the formation of glaciers, occur atop high peaks in tropical Ecuador and at several other locations on or near the equator.

A Six-month Night

Polar World peoples experience a "six-month night." The six-month night (followed by a six-month day) occurs only at 90 degrees north and south latitudes. No one lives at either pole, of course. In fact, very few people live north of the 75th parallel. At this latitude, even on the shortest day (December 21 in the Northern Hemisphere), daytime twilight provides light for most outdoor activities. Admittedly, throughout most of the Polar World, winter days are very short and nights are very long.

TEMPERATURE

Many factors combine to determine a location's temperature conditions. In the case of the Polar World, several controls stand out as being particularly influential. The following discussion focuses upon three aspects of temperature: controls, conditions, and related phenomena.

Controls
Latitude

The word *climate* comes from a Greek word meaning "slope." In equatorial latitudes, incoming sunlight strikes Earth's surface directly. At poleward latitudes, however, it strikes the sloping surface at an angle. The same amount of incoming solar energy is concentrated in tropical latitudes, but it is spread over a much greater area near the poles. This is the primary reason Earth's poleward areas are colder.

Duration of Sunlight

As long as the sun is above the horizon, it is heating Earth's surface. After it sets, the source of heat is gone, heat radiates back into space, and cooling begins to occur. With the long duration of summer sunlight experienced at high latitudes, temperatures can become surprisingly high (although not in areas of polar ice cap). The direct opposite can be said for winter cold. You must remember that the sun is always above and below the horizon for one-half of the year. The difference is duration. At the equator, the intervals are 12 hours above and 12 hours below the horizon every day of the year. At the poles, the duration is six consecutive months above the horizon, followed by six months of darkness. The Arctic and Antarctic circles (66 1/2 degrees north and south latitudes, respectively) are the points at which the sun will not rise one day or set one day during the year. If a location receives 21 hours of sunlight on a particular date during the summer, it is balanced by 21 hours of darkness six months later during the winter.

Land and Water Distribution

Land heats and cools faster and to greater extremes than does water. During both summer and winter seasons, air temperatures may vary by 50 or more degrees Fahrenheit (30°C) during a single day, but a nearby lake or river may experience little if any change in temperature. The closer a land location is to a large body of water, the less apt it is to experience high or low temperature extremes. This can be illustrated by temperature differences at two Alaska locations: Nome (on the Pacific coast) and Fairbanks (in the interior), both of which lie at approximately the same latitude (see table on the following

Location	Lowest mo. avg.	Highest mo. avg.	Extreme low	Extreme high
Nome	6 (–15°C)	51 (11°C)	–54 (–48°C)	86 (28°C)
Fairbanks	–10 (–23°C)	62 (16°C)	–66 (–54°C)	89 (31°C)

page). The impact of land and water on temperatures can be seen throughout the Polar World. Coldest winter and warmest summer temperatures occur in continental interiors.

Other Influences

Several other factors influence temperatures on a more local basis. Ocean currents play a significant role in those areas of Alaska that face the northern Pacific and the warm Alaska Current. The same holds true in the North Atlantic, where southern Greenland, Iceland, and coastal Norway are bathed by the warm waters of the North Atlantic Drift (the northward extension of the Gulf Stream).

Elevation also plays a very important role in influencing temperatures. Under normal conditions, atmospheric temperatures drop about 3.5°F with each 1,000-foot (2°C per 300-meter) increase in elevation. In the Polar World, however, few people live in mountains, so this control is of little consequence in human terms. Mountains do play an important role, however, in contributing to air drainage. Cold air chilled by high elevations is denser and therefore heavier than warm air. As a result, it tends to "flow" (as wind) into lower elevations, where it "ponds," just as water does flowing into a basin. Many of the world's coldest temperatures, including in the Arctic region, have been recorded in basins surrounded by mountains.

Surface color also makes a difference in temperatures. A white surface of ice or snow reflects incoming sunlight back into space, resulting in lower temperatures. A dark surface such as bare rock or soil, on the other hand, will absorb sunlight, resulting in warmer temperatures.

Conditions

As is true within the midlatitudes, as well as in the Arctic, July or August is usually the warmest month and January or February the coldest. Summers are very short, and winters are very long and monotonous. As you would imagine, a number of record temperature extremes have occurred in the Polar World.

The coldest temperature ever recorded under natural conditions was an unbelievable 129°F below zero (–89°C) in Antarctica in July 1983 (remember, seasons are reversed in the respective hemispheres). Fortunately, no one lives at this location! (The freezer in most home refrigerators is set at about 0°F [–17°C].) Verkhoyansk, located in the continental interior of eastern Siberia (67 degrees north latitude, 133 degrees east longitude), holds several rather unenviable weather records, including the possibility of being the world's coldest inhabited community. For the latter "honor," it vies with another Siberian community, Oymyakon, where in 1926 the temperature dropped to a shivering –96°F (–71.2°C). In Verkhoyansk, in 1961, however, the temperature unofficially (although recorded under official conditions) dropped to a tooth-chattering –102°F (–74°C).

At the opposite extreme, Verkhoyansk also once recorded a temperature of 100°F (40°C). (It should be noted that little agreement exists on figures for either high or low extremes, so they should be considered approximate only.) This span gave the town yet another amazing weather record—a range of 202 degrees Fahrenheit (116°C) between its highest and lowest temperatures! Monthly averages in Verkhoyansk are also startling. No inhabited spot on Earth can match the village's January temperature average of –59°F (–51°C). (By comparison, International Falls, Minnesota, which brags of being "The Nation's Ice Box," has a January average of 2°F [–17°C].) With a 60°F (15°C) July average, the range between warmest and coldest month in Verkhoyansk is 119°F (67°C)—also a world record!

Verkhoyansk experiences bone-chilling record cold and amazing temperature extremes because it is located in a low-elevation basin surrounded by mountains on three sides. Cold air from the high mountains pours into the valley, where a community of about 1,800 people is located. It is also located far inland, well out of reach of any possible temperature-moderating influence of either the Arctic or Pacific oceans. Elsewhere in the Polar World, Greenland has experienced a record low temperature of –87°F (–66°C). Alaska's record low is –80°F (–62°C), recorded in 1971 at Prospect Creek Camp, located along the Alaska pipeline, about 20 miles (32 kilometers) north of the Arctic Circle. This is a scant one degree warmer than North America's record low of –81°F (–63°C), recorded in 1947 at Snag, Yukon, Canada.

"Hot" rarely comes to mind when one thinks about the Polar World! You must remember, however, the influence of duration (how long the sun shines) on temperatures. Long summer days can become quite hot and even miserable to people accustomed to cold. In Alaska's Kobuk Desert, located just north of the Arctic Circle, an unofficial temperature of 109°F (43°C) has been recorded (but, in terms of equipment, under official conditions). Although rare, Alaska, Canada, and Siberia have all recorded temperatures in the 90s°F (upper 30s° C) and some locations have reached 100°F (40°C).

Temperature-related Phenomena

It may surprise you to learn that, for most Polar World natives winter is the preferred season! The brief summer brings warmth, but it also brings buzzing swarms of irritating insects that make life miserable for both man and beast. In addition, travel can be extremely difficult if not impossible across a surface covered by mud, thousands of lakes, and numerous streams after the spring thaw. During the winter season, the insects are gone, and food is stored from summer hunting and gathering. Transportation is relatively easy on the frozen earth, snow, or ice surfaces. This is the season when people gather to socialize and when settlement is stationary rather than migratory. When the air is calm, outdoor activities continue

Ice fog is made up of tiny ice crystals caused by car exhaust, which generally occurs when the temperature dips below 14°F (–10°C). Pictured here is a vehicle driving through ice fog in Fairbanks, Alaska, during a record-breaking cold snap in January 2006.

until temperatures drop into the –40 to –50°F (–40 to –46°C) range.

Severely cold temperatures cause rather strange things to happen. A cup of hot beverage tossed into the air will freeze before hitting the ground. Metal becomes brittle and can break. Vehicles are kept running to prevent fuel and oil from freezing solid. Vehicle exhaust causes dense ice fog that can cut visibility to almost zero. When a person exhales, breath instantly freezes into ice crystals. Eyes involuntarily water and tears freeze instantly. Exposed flesh can freeze in seconds. In cold, clear, calm weather, sounds such as human voices or barking dogs can be heard clearly many miles from their source (be careful what you say!). Temperature inversions (a layer of cold air underlying upper warmer air) can create an optical illusion in which distant objects located below the horizon appear above the horizon. Depth perception, particularly on cloudy or foggy days, is nearly impossible. Snow, ice, and sky all blend together, resulting in "white-out" conditions. When this occurs, the horizon vanishes, and even walking can be difficult.

Many scientists are deeply concerned over the rapid climatic change occurring in the Arctic. Data suggest that the region is warming twice as quickly as the rest of the planet. With warming, glaciers melt, ecosystems change, frozen ground thaws, and many other conditions occur that severely threaten the environment and human settlement and activity.

PRECIPITATION

Precipitation is any form of falling moisture—rain, snow, hail, or sleet. Conditions that create hail and sleet rarely if ever occur in colder portions of the Polar World. Most of the region's moisture falls in the form of rain or snow. With regard to Polar World precipitation, two things stand out. First, and perhaps surprisingly, half to two-thirds of all precipitation (other than on the ice caps) falls as summer rain. Most locations receive very little snow. Second, with the exception of more southerly regions of the subarctic climate, at least by one definition, the region is classified as a "desert."

Controls

Deserts are defined in several ways, only one of which applies to the Polar World. It is difficult, after all, to believe that a region with hundreds of thousands of lakes, many huge rivers, and vast snowfields and glaciers could be classified as a desert!

Most climatologists (scientists who study the atmosphere) define deserts as locations with a moisture deficit. That is, not enough moisture is received to make up for the potential loss through evaporation, thereby leaving conditions very dry. Certainly this condition does not apply to any portion of the Polar World. Another definition of deserts, however, does: regions receiving less than 10 inches (25 centimeters) of precipitation annually. By this definition, nearly all the Polar World is, indeed, a desert.

At poleward latitudes, precipitation is scant for five reasons. First, because of the region's constantly cool to cold temperatures, little moisture evaporates from the surface into the atmosphere. As a result, the air is quite dry. Second, the prevailing wind system between 60 and 90 degrees of latitude is generally northerly; that is, it blows from north to south. As this occurs, the air warms as it moves southward into lower latitudes during the summer months. Warming air increases its moisture-holding capacity, rather than losing its moisture as precipitation. Third, because of the cold, convectional thundershowers are rare throughout much of the region. In this process, heated air rises and is cooled (which is necessary for precipitation to occur). Convection is responsible for the summer thundershowers in some warmer inland locations. Fourth, moisture-bearing warm air masses from the tropics and subtropics that contribute to precipitation to the middle latitudes rarely reach the Polar World. Finally, most of the region is overlain by a semipermanent high-pressure system, resulting in a very stable atmosphere. (This condition occurs in the midlatitudes on very clear, calm, crisp winter days.)

Conditions

Although much of the Polar World receives little precipitation, the amount varies. In portions of the region, only a few inches of moisture falls each year. The driest location is the interior of Antarctica, which receives about 2 inches (5 centimeters)—all of which falls as snow. It should be noted that precipitation figures are always given in water equivalent, so the "2" figure is actually the water content of melted snow.

Throughout most of the subpolar region, annual precipitation averages 4 to 6 inches (10 to 15 centimeters). Barrow, Alaska, receives on average 4.5 inches (11.5 centimeters) of

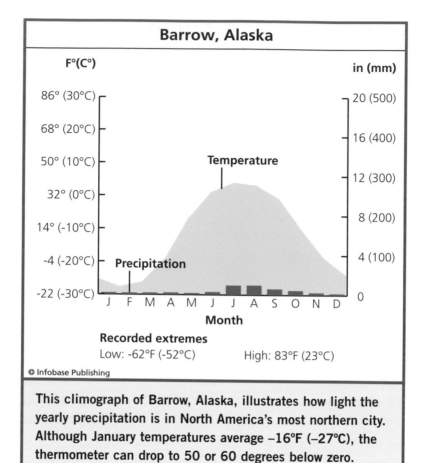

Barrow, Alaska

F°(C°) | in (mm)

86° (30°C) — | — 20 (500)
68° (20°C) — | — 16 (400)
50° (10°C) — |
32° (0°C) — | — 12 (300)
14° (-10°C) — | — 8 (200)
-4 (-20°C) — | — 4 (100)
-22 (-30°C) — | 0

Temperature

Precipitation

J F M A M J J A S O N D

Month

Recorded extremes
Low: -62°F (-52°C)   High: 83°F (23°C)

© Infobase Publishing

This climograph of Barrow, Alaska, illustrates how light the yearly precipitation is in North America's most northern city. Although January temperatures average –16°F (–27°C), the thermometer can drop to 50 or 60 degrees below zero.

moisture, 60 percent of which falls as summer rain. The city receives only about 20 inches (50 centimeters) of winter snow. Most communities in Siberia, including Verkhoyansk, average about 5 inches (13 centimeters) of precipitation, more than 75 percent of which falls from June through August as rain. The highest amounts of precipitation (including snow) occur in warmer areas where evaporation is greater, resulting in the atmosphere containing more moisture. These conditions are found on the southern margins of the Subarctic region and in areas bordering the northern reaches of the Atlantic and Pacific oceans.

OTHER WEATHER ELEMENTS AND CONDITIONS

Wind and fog are two atmospheric conditions common to many, though not all, areas of the Arctic. Antarctica is one of the windiest places on Earth. Sustained winds of 150 to 200 miles per hour (250 to 325 kilometers per hour) have been recorded on the continent. In the North American Arctic, the highest winds occur in northern and eastern Canada. In Eurasia, they are most common along the Arctic coastal fringe.

Wind is significant for two primary reasons. First, it combines with temperature to determine the temperature your body actually feels (see chart on page 31). Second, blowing snow limits visibility. When the air is cold, snow falls as small, fine crystals that are easily blown about by even a slight breeze. When winds exceed 12 to 15 miles per hour (19 to 24 kilometers per hour), surface drifting begins. Higher wind velocities will create blizzard conditions, in which snow is blown many feet off the ground. Under such conditions, visibility can drop to zero. In areas of greatest wind and snow accumulation, blowing snow can obscure visibility up to 100 days a year.

Fog (a cloud in contact with the ground) also is common to many areas, particularly those located near water. It occurs under several conditions. First is the previously mentioned ice fog, created under conditions of extreme cold and calm winds. Moisture from vehicle exhausts, chimneys, or industrial sources immediately freezes, creating a dense fog of minute ice crystals. In urban areas such as Fairbanks, Alaska, ice fog is frequent and can reduce visibility to near zero. A second type is radiation fog (or ground fog), formed when moisture in air overlying a colder surface condenses (clouds and fog are forms of condensed moisture). It is most common on cool, clear, summer nights with little wind. Advection fog is a third type that is common to the region. Advection refers to the horizontal movement of air. If warm, moist air moves across a colder surface, condensation can occur, resulting in fog. This condition frequently exists along coasts, where warmer moist air moves inland across the colder land surface. Coastal Barrow, Alaska, for example, experiences fog an average 210 days a year! Another type of advection fog is "sea smoke," a type unique to polar waters. It forms when much colder air drifts across relatively warm water. In appearance, the low bank resembles smoke rising from the water.

Dryness and cold greatly slow organic decay. Driftwood will remain along a shore for decades. Along the treeless Arctic coast, the availability of driftwood can be a matter of life or death if needed for fuel, building, or repair. Among native people, there has long been an unwritten law: If a piece of driftwood is found above the strand line (the line where waves deposit debris), it means that someone moved it there. By custom, the wood is left alone, because it may eventually be desperately needed by the person who moved it. Meat remains

Determining Wind Chill

As most readers know, freezing temperatures can be quite pleasant on a clear, calm day. On the other hand, the same temperature accompanied by a howling wind can create absolute misery. This condition is known as the "windchill" temperature, or the temperature your body actually feels. Windchill is based on a formula that takes into consideration temperature and wind velocity. For example, if the temperature is 30°F (–1°C), and the wind is blowing 30 miles per hour (42 kilometers per hour), it will actually feel like 15°F (–9.5°C). If you know the wind speed and temperature, you can use the following chart to determine how cold your body thinks it is!

* Chart adapted from the National Weather Service. Available online at http://www.crh.noaa.gov/ddc/windchill.php.

Windchill Chart

Temperature (°F)

	40	35	30	25	20	15	10	5	0	-5	-10	-15	-20	-25	-30	-35	-40	-45
Calm	40	35	30	25	20	15	10	5	0	-5	-10	-15	-20	-25	-30	-35	-40	-45
5	36	31	25	19	13	7	1	-5	-11	-16	-22	-28	-34	-40	-46	-52	-57	-63
10	34	27	21	15	9	3	-4	-10	-16	-22	-28	-35	-41	-47	-53	-59	-66	-72
15	32	25	19	13	6	0	-7	-13	-19	-26	-32	-39	-45	-51	-58	-64	-71	-77
20	30	24	17	11	4	-2	-9	-15	-22	-29	-35	-42	-48	-55	-61	-68	-74	-81
25	29	23	16	9	3	-4	-11	-17	-24	-31	-37	-44	-51	-58	-64	-71	-78	-84
30	28	22	15	8	1	-5	-12	-19	-26	-33	-39	-46	-53	-60	-67	-73	-80	-87
35	28	21	14	7	0	-7	-14	-21	-27	-34	-41	-48	-55	-62	-69	-76	-82	-89
40	27	20	13	6	-1	-8	-15	-22	-29	-36	-43	-50	-57	-64	-71	-78	-84	-91
45	26	19	12	5	-2	-9	-16	-23	-30	-37	-44	-51	-58	-65	-72	-79	-86	-93
50	26	19	12	4	-3	-10	-17	-24	-31	-38	-45	-52	-60	-67	-74	-81	-88	-95
55	25	18	11	4	-3	-11	-18	-25	-32	-39	-46	-54	-61	-68	-75	-82	-89	-97
60	25	17	10	3	-4	-11	-19	-26	-33	-40	-48	-55	-62	-69	-76	-84	-91	-98

Frostbite occurs in 15 minutes or less

Windchill is the still-air temperature that would have the same cooling effect on exposed human skin as a given combination of temperature and wind speed. This chart illustrates how cold it actually feels in relation to how hard the wind is blowing (wind speeds are listed in the far left column).

The aurora borealis, or northern lights, is a common occurrence in the Polar Regions. The lights are typically seen in the northern sky when electrons collide with atoms in the upper atmosphere. Pictured here is the aurora borealis in the sky above Eagle River, Alaska.

fresh indefinitely. There are even many accounts of woolly mammoth carcasses—extinct for some 10,000 years—being discovered buried in ice or frozen ground and the flesh being fresh and eaten!

NORTHERN LIGHTS

Although not associated with weather and climate, the aurora borealis, or northern lights, is one of nature's most spectacular displays. (The equivalent in the Southern Hemisphere is the aurora australis.) Occasionally, an aurora is seen in the mid-latitudes, but it is a common occurrence in the Polar World, where it may appear more than 300 nights a year. The magnificent displays most frequently appear as ribbons or curtains of lights dancing about, high in the heavens. They are often white, but can appear in nearly any color or variety of colors. For spectacular views of the aurora and additional information on the phenomenon, visit the NASA Web site. (For this and other recommendations, see "Web sites" in the back of this book.) In the following chapter, you will learn how conditions of the Polar World's weather and climate have affected the region's hydrosphere—its waters in the form of snow, ice, and frozen ground.

3

Snow, Ice, and Frozen Ground

The primary direct effect of low polar temperatures is the dominance of snow, ice, and permafrost (permanently frozen ground) on Polar World landscapes. These elements are also of great importance to people living in the Arctic. People of various cultures recognize and name things that are important to them. Many Americans recognize frozen moisture by only two words: *snow* and *ice*. Each of these may be labeled, in turn, as one of several subtypes, such as "slush" and "drift" for snow. Because of their great significance to native polar cultures, however, a great many different terms are used to identify and label different conditions of snow and ice. The number of categories and types, and therefore words, varies by language and dialect. Some studies suggest that several hundred words exist. The Inuit, for example, have up to 12 to 15 categories of ice and snow, further divided into 80 to 100 subtypes. Such numbers, themselves, are of little significance. What is important is what they tell us about the significance of snow and ice to native Arctic cultures.

SNOW

Snow is one of the most conspicuous features of the Arctic landscape. In places, it covers both land and the frozen sea throughout much of the year. As you learned in the previous chapter, its prevalence is not the result of huge amounts of snowfall. Rather, the scant amount of snow that does fall remains on the surface for seven to nine months. In most Arctic locations, snow can fall during every month of the year. Amazingly, Barrow, Alaska, receives more snow in July than Thule (located in northwestern Greenland) does in January or February! In fact, more snow falls during summer than winter months in Greenland and northern portions of the Canadian Archipelago (Arctic islands).

Under conditions of extreme cold, much of the snow falls as needles, or fine crystals. Because of their small size and light weight, they are more easily blown about than are the larger, wetter flakes with which most readers are familiar. As a result, in some areas as much as 75 to 90 percent of the Arctic surface may be relatively snow-free. Other than in the densely forested taiga region, deep snow is generally limited to places where it drifts on the leeward (downwind) side of obstacles or fills deep depressions. Blizzards (blowing snow) create hazardous conditions that restrict many human activities in polar lands. Wind-blown snow creates "white-out" conditions that severely limit visibility and can cause people to become disoriented easily. Surfaces tend to be leveled out as snow is swept from exposed flat surfaces and deposited in depressions. One can easily step on one of these "snow pits" and immediately sink out of sight!

Snow accumulations have long been of use to native cultures and others. Where wind action has packed the snow, giving it a hard surface, the combination of frozen ground, hardpack (snow), and ice cover is ideal for travel. Such surfaces also accommodate aircraft landings. Packed snow has been used as a building material, best recognized by the Inuit (Eskimo) igloo. Melted snow provides water for human and animal consumption. In this context, it should be noted that humans are unable to provide adequate fluid for their bodies by melting snow in the mouth. Doing so freezes the oral cavity, causing pain and severe membrane damage.

ICE

Ice is the dominant surface cover throughout much of the polar realm. It covers about 6 million square miles (15.5 million square kilometers) of Antarctica, Greenland, and scattered smaller areas. The combined land surface covered by ice is roughly twice that of the combined lower 48 U.S. states. Ice covers most of the Arctic Ocean throughout the year and all of it during the winter months. The region's lakes, rivers, gulfs, seas, and bays are also ice covered much of the year. Ice associated with water bodies is formed from the direct freezing of water. Glacial ice, on the other hand, forms gradually from compacted snow and over a much longer period of time. In the following section, ice cover is discussed under three different categories: glacial ice caps and ice sheets, mountain glaciers, and sea ice.

Glacial Ice Caps and Ice Sheets

Ice caps and ice sheets (also called continental glaciers) differ only in size—ice caps being much larger in area and thickness than the smaller ice sheets. All glacial ice forms from compacted snow. Many readers are familiar with the process in which a snowball, under further compaction, turns into a ball of ice. If more snow falls and accumulates than is lost through melting, runoff, and evaporation, it will begin to accumulate. As long as the accumulation continues year after year, new layers are added. Gradually, the weight of the overlying snow begins to compact lower layers, and glacial ice begins to form. When less snow falls than is lost to the atmosphere or melt and runoff, a glacier begins to ablate, or shrink in size.

On four occasions in the geologic past—during the Pleistocene (ice age) geologic epoch—huge masses of glacial

The Greenland ice cap—the world's second largest—contains one-eighth of the world's ice. In 2006, it was reported that the ice cap was melting twice as fast as it was in 2001.

ice covered most of the Arctic and all of Antarctica. These ice caps began retreating approximately 20,000 years ago, but there are remnants that serve as reminders of this much colder period of Earth's history. In fact, in Antarctica, scientists have drilled ice cores that reveal up to 740,000 years of climatic history! The largest remnant is the huge Antarctic ice cap, which covers nearly the entire continent, an area of about 5.4 million square miles (14 million square kilometers). Most of the thousand or so scientists stationed in Antarctica are there seeking to unlock the secrets of the world's largest ice mass and to better understand its environmental effects. Otherwise, the continent's frigid temperatures and ice-covered surfaces form an inhospitable environment in which no plant or animal life, or permanent human settlement, has taken root.

In the Northern Hemisphere, Pleistocene ice caps were centered over northern Canada and Eurasia. From their centers, they spread to cover vast areas of North America and the huge Eurasian landmass. In the United States, lobes of glacial ice crept southward as far as the present-day Ohio and Missouri river valleys. Acting as giant bulldozers, the relentlessly flowing ice scoured land, eroding some areas and depositing its till (glacial debris) elsewhere. This finely pulverized glacial debris eventually became the parent material from which much of the rich soil of the U.S. Corn Belt was formed. In both North America and Eurasia, glacially scoured basins and trenches were later occupied by hundreds of thousands of lakes, including the North America Great Lakes system.

Today, ice caps cover nearly all of Greenland. Smaller ice sheets occur on some islands of the Canadian Archipelago and in Iceland. The Columbia Icefield, a 125-square-mile (325-square-kilometer) ice sheet is the southernmost such feature in North America. It is tucked away in the Rocky Mountains of British Columbia, near Jasper National Park.

Glaciers flow, just like water, although at a snail's pace. They have a core, or center, usually the point at which the ice is deepest. Under the weight and pressure of this "ice dome," the ice mass moves outward. This process can be illustrated by pouring a chilled, thick liquid, such as syrup, onto a flat surface and watching it flow slowly outward. Theoretically, movement would be outward in all directions and at the same speed. In reality, however, terrain plays a major role in the direction and speed of glacial movement. Features such as mountains and valleys, as well as slope and gravity, influence glacial flow.

When glaciers flow into the sea, large chunks of ice break off. This process, called calving, is the source of icebergs. These huge masses of ice are often swept by currents into oceanic shipping lanes. Just as an ice cube is nearly submerged in a glass of liquid, so, too, are icebergs submerged in the ocean. Only about one-eighth of their mass is above water, leaving the rest below and out of sight, as a potential hazard. In

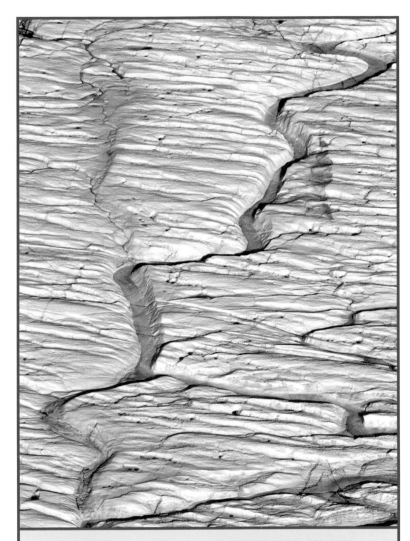

In Greenland, glaciers are increasingly flowing out of the fjords toward the open sea. The patterns in this glacier indicate that the ice is being pressed away from Greenland and in the process rivers are appearing in the ice.

1912, the Titanic was sunk in the North Atlantic when it collided with an iceberg that had probably drifted southward from Greenland. The ship was the largest cruise vessel in the world at the time and was built to be unsinkable. Sink it did, however, taking an estimated 1,500 people to a watery grave on the ocean floor in one of the greatest nonmilitary marine disasters in history.

Glaciers contain about 75 percent of Earth's freshwater, most of which is locked up in the massive ice caps and ice sheets. Scientists know that during the last ice age, when nearly one-third of all land was covered by glaciers, sea level was 400 to 450 feet (120 to 140 meters) lower than it is today. Were the existing glacial ice to melt, the sea level would rise another estimated 230 feet (70 meters). The results to low-lying settle-ments, which include most of the world's great cities, would be catastrophic. This is just one of the many concerns that geographers and others have in regard to Earth's warming temperatures.

Mountain or Alpine Glaciers

Mountain glaciers, as the name suggests, are glaciers formed at high elevations. They are also called alpine glaciers, because scientists first studied these features in Europe's high Alps. Unlike ice caps, they are not confined to polar latitudes. In fact, these smaller glaciers actually occur at high elevations in the equatorial latitudes! They are formed, however, by the same processes that create larger glaciers. As snow accumulates, its increasing weight compacts the layers of snow below, gradu-ally changing them into glacial ice. If more moisture is received in the form of snow than is lost to evaporation and melting, the glacier will grow. If, on the other hand, more moisture is lost than is received, the glacier will recede. Today, throughout much of the polar realm and elsewhere, glaciers are receding, some of them at an alarming rate.

Sea Ice

Sea ice includes all features involving frozen seawater. In terms of area covered, it is the most widespread: It is composed of most of the Arctic Ocean, as well as the ocean immediately surrounding Antarctica. In the Arctic, by late winter, when sea ice reaches its maximum extent, it creeps southward to about 60 degrees north latitude. Exceptions are found in those areas of the North Atlantic that are bathed by warm water currents. During summer months, the ice retreats poleward. Some areas remain ice covered year-round. These include most of the Arctic Ocean Basin, the waters off northern Greenland, and some straits in the northern reaches of the Canadian Archipelago.

Scientists identify a number of different types of sea ice, based on the way it is formed. Fast ice (also called shelf ice) is stationary ice that grows outward from shorelines, as temperatures begin dropping below freezing on a regular basis. Floe ice consists of detached fragments of floating sea ice. These floating sheets of thin ice move and may be separated by leads, or areas of open water. Pack ice (or drift ice) is formed by the joining of many ice floes, leaving little if any open water. Ice packs cover large areas, measured by hundreds or even thousands of square miles, and are constantly on the move.

Ice islands are found in both the Arctic and the Antarctic regions. They are huge masses of floating ice that have broken away from coastal fast ice or an ice shelf. One ice island, called "B-15," broke off from Antarctica's Ross Ice Shelf in 2000. Its surface area is about 4,500 square miles (11,655 square kilometers), slightly smaller than the state of Connecticut. It is believed to contain enough freshwater to supply the United States for five years! (Salt is removed from sea ice within a period of about one year.) Many smaller ice islands are found in the Arctic Basin. They move with the ocean's currents at a rate of about one mile (1.6 kilometers) a day and complete a circumpolar route in about nine years. Because they are large, stable, and moving, a number of the ice islands have been used as scientific research stations by Americans, Russians, and others. Finally, there is the polar ice of the central Arctic Ocean.

Smooth ice is easily traversed, which is one reason why native peoples prefer the winter season. In some locations, however, particularly near coasts, ice tends to be very rugged and difficult to traverse. Jagged surfaces are created in several ways. The most common are tidal action and ice jamming. Where tidal range is measured in feet, ice is broken into pieces, which tend to pile up and form a very irregular surface. Elsewhere, ice jams are formed as moving masses of ice collide. Such terrain, featuring sharp ridges, jumbled masses, and reaches of open water, can be difficult if not impossible to cross. At sea, thick ice limits navigation. With rapidly warming temperatures and ever more powerful icebreaking ships, the Arctic "Mediterranean" may soon be turned into a valuable shipping route!

Lake and River Ice

As a percentage of total area covered, the polar region has more fresh surface water than any other part of the world. On relatively flat terrain, about 40 to 60 percent of the surface is water covered and in some areas much more. Throughout most of the region, lakes and rivers remain frozen for 8 to 10 months of the year. For humans, the smooth ice creates an ideal surface for travel by dog sled or snowmobile, as well as aircraft take-offs and landings. Arctic winds tend to keep the ice snow-free, which further facilitates travel.

PERMAFROST

It seems strange that one of the major problems facing the Arctic region is the threat of warming temperatures, which cause frozen ground to thaw. This is the case, though, throughout nearly the entire region. Within the Polar World (and beyond), few if any environmental conditions pose a greater threat than does the loss of permanently frozen ground. As anyone living in colder areas of the United States or Canada knows, ground freezes solid during the winter. As winter cold gradually gives way to warmer springtime temperatures, the ground begins to thaw. In warm areas, all of the frozen ground thaws. Where winters are long and extremely cold, and summers very short, however, only the surface layer thaws, which creates an upper active layer of earth. Beneath the active layer, ground remains frozen. This condition of permanently frozen ground is called permafrost.

Permafrost underlies an estimated 25 percent of Earth's land surface. It affects most of Alaska and about half of both Canada and Russia. It even reaches into the northern Rocky Mountains, as far south as Colorado. Temperatures and the length of summer are the chief factors in determining the thickness of the active layer. Basically, the colder the temperatures and shorter the summer, the thinner the active layer and the thicker the zone of permafrost. Depending on temperature conditions, the active layer may be several inches to as much as 10 feet (3 meters) deep. Below the active layer, permafrost can vary from a few feet in thickness to great depths. In Barrow, Alaska, permafrost extends to about 1,300 feet (400 meters). Near Verkhoyansk, Siberia, it is 4,800 feet (1,463 meters) thick. Distribution of permafrost is continuous in colder areas of the Arctic. Southward, as conditions warm, its occurrence becomes discontinuous or sporadic (scattered).

Permafrost influences many conditions, both natural and human. Trees, for example, cannot take root in a thin active layer. Permafrost, therefore, is a major factor in determining the distribution of forests and size of forest trees. Some landforms are influenced by permafrost. Many human activities also are affected by both the permanently frozen ground and the overlying active layer. Sanitary systems and water supplies, for example, must be built to overcome the problem of ground that remains frozen throughout the year. On the other hand, storage rooms cut into the permafrost make wonderful refrigerators!

Engineered and constructed works are extremely vulnerable to the alternate freezing and thawing of the ground. Imagine constructing a building, road, railroad, landing strip, or other structure on a solid foundation (such as cement or permanently frozen ground). Obviously, it would be stable. What happens, though, if these features are built on a surface

A muskeg is a boggy surface of poorly drained land with a heavy accumulation of organic material. Pictured here is a muskeg in Yukon Territory, Canada, which is surrounded by spruce trees and other tundra vegetation.

that thaws out and turns into a mushy, spongy mess during part of the year? As the active layer thaws, structures begin to sink into the ooze. *Muskeg* is the term given to boggy surfaces of poorly drained land with a heavy accumulation of organic material. (Because of the cold, organic material decomposes very slowly in the Arctic.) On such surfaces, transportation routes begin to heave here and sink there, as the ground begins to thaw beneath them in places. How can these conditions be avoided?

Several methods have been developed to minimize permafrost damage to structures. One is to build a large "mat" upon which light buildings, roadways, or airstrips can then be built. Another is to remove the active layer all the way down to the permafrost and replace it with solid material such as gravel. A third means, most commonly used in building and bridge construction, is to create a foundation by inserting pilings deeply into the permafrost layer, thereby stabilizing them. In some instances, the frozen ground is even preserved using refrigeration. Much of Alaska's Dalton Highway to Prudhoe Bay was built over an insulating bed of fiberglass. All these methods, of course, add greatly to construction time and cost. In fact, building across permafrost can increase construction costs fourfold.

If temperatures continue to warm in areas underlain by permafrost, the active layer will greatly increase in thickness. Mats will begin to sink beneath the weight of the structures they support. Rock fill and pilings will be inadequate, as the permafrost melts away beneath them. Artificially freezing a greatly expanded active layer will become cost prohibitive. This is much more than an idle concern of scientists. Remember, one-fourth of Earth's surface is underlain by permafrost. This includes nearly every building, highway, railroad, and airstrip in Alaska, as well as those in half of Canada and Russia! Damages and prevention costs easily could amount to hundreds of billions of dollars.

We will return to conditions of snow, ice, and permafrost. You will learn how they have affected other aspects of the natural environment and how humans have adapted to these seemingly harsh natural elements.

4

Landforms
and Ecosystems

As is true of most other geographic aspects of the Polar World, the primary agent contributing to the region's unique landforms and ecosystems can be expressed in a single word: temperature. There are, of course, many other elements at work, but none comes close to matching low temperatures as the dominant force shaping the region's landforms, plant and animal life, soils, and freshwater features.

LANDFORMS

Landform features range in size from huge continental landmasses and ocean basins to features as small as the land on which one is standing. At a continental scale, the Polar World includes Antarctica and spans the northern portions of North America and Eurasia. Viewed from above the North Pole, the 5.5-million-square-mile (15,250,000-square-kilometer) Arctic Ocean Basin is the most prominent feature; it is also the most centrally located within the

Arctic region. With an area of about 840,000 square miles (2,175,000 square kilometers), Greenland is the world's largest island. Elsewhere, scattered through the North Pacific and North Atlantic basins and the Arctic Ocean are various island groups, the largest being the Canadian Archipelago.

Landform Regions

At the next level are features such as mountains, platcaus, hills, and plains, each of which occurs within the region. The highest mountain within the Polar World (and all of North America) is Alaska's majestic Mount McKinley, or Denali. This spectacular peak rises 20,320 feet (6,194 meters) above the surrounding plains, which are near sea level. No mountain in the world can match its vertical rise from base to peak in such a close horizontal distance. Several peaks in Alaska's Brooks Range exceed 8,000 feet (2,500 meters), the tallest being snow- and glacier-covered Mount Michelson, with an elevation of 9,239 feet (2,816 meters). Greenland's highest elevation is atop 12,139-foot (3,700-meter) Mount Gunnbjorn. Like many of the island's other peaks, it barely reaches above the island's thick blanket of glacial ice. Much of eastern Siberia is a rugged land of mountains, plateaus, and hills. Although only one peak barely reaches above 10,000 feet (3,050 meters), the combined terrain and severe cold make cross-country travel within the region all but impossible. No road or railroad crosses the area.

Much of the region's topography is dominated by very flat plains. The largest is the Western Siberian Lowland, located just to the east of Russia's Ural Mountains. Occupying an area of about one million square miles (2.6 million square kilometers), it is the world's largest expanse of unbroken lowland and swamp. Elsewhere, portions of the great North European Plain extend northward into the Polar World. In North America, plains cover much of the area around Hudson Bay and also large expanses of the coastal regions of Alaska and Canada. For 8 to 10 months a year, all land and water surfaces are locked in the frozen grip of winter. It is during this long season that the

The highest mountain within the Polar World is Mount McKinley, or Denali, which is located in south-central Alaska's Denali National Park. Mount McKinley is North America's highest mountain at 20,320 feet (6,194 meters) and has the world's highest vertical rise (18,000 feet, or 5,486 meters).

plains can be easily traversed by dog sledge, snowmobile, or other means of Arctic travel.

Effects of Glaciation

Throughout the region, glacial ice has been the primary agent at work in shaping the land. Huge continental ice masses tended to level terrain, removing surface material in one location, transporting it hundreds if not thousands of miles, and depositing it in another. Where ice age masses grew to depths of several miles, the overlying weight of the ice actually forced the land downward. The basins occupied by Europe's North Sea, Asia's Western Siberian Lowland, and North America's

Hudson Bay were all formed in this way. As the burden of ice is removed—over time intervals measured by thousands of years—the land slowly rises, or "rebounds."

When deposited, glacial till (rock debris) takes many forms. Eskers—long, low ridges of sand and gravel—can snake for many miles across the terrain. Drumlins are smaller depositional features that are half-egg-shaped in form. Their highest point indicates the direction from which the glacier came, and elevation descends in the direction of movement. On the glacial margins, terminal moraines are formed where the till is deposited. This unconsolidated material may be very fine, or it may contain boulders transported hundreds of miles before they are dumped. These rocks are called glacial erratics. They litter the ground's surface in the Upper Midwest and New England, where they pose a great problem to farmers. Stones must be removed from fields, or they will damage plowshares and other equipment. Occasionally, boulders the size of houses can be found in fields! Lakes and many short rivers with deranged drainage patterns are among the most obvious glacial features of the north.

Mountain glaciers, unlike continental ice sheets, tend to increase relief, or the ruggedness of terrain. Because of their sculpting action, anyplace in the world where Alpine glaciers have formed (now or in the past) will show telltale signs of their chiseling, erosive force. They leave a rugged and distinctive imprint on the mountainous landscapes they create. Skiers are familiar with the term bowl, basins in which deep powder snow often accumulates. Most bowls are cirques, the pockets shaped by and in which mountain glaciers form. When cirques form on opposite sides of a mountain ridge, they form a variety of rugged features. Among the better-known forms are horns (as the famous Matterhorn in the Swiss Alps), arêtes (sawtooth-like ridges, as can be seen in Grand Teton National Park, in Wyoming), and cols (valleys).

From their source, glaciers flow slowly downslope, scouring a U-shaped valley in their path. When they cut below

Postglacial Landforms

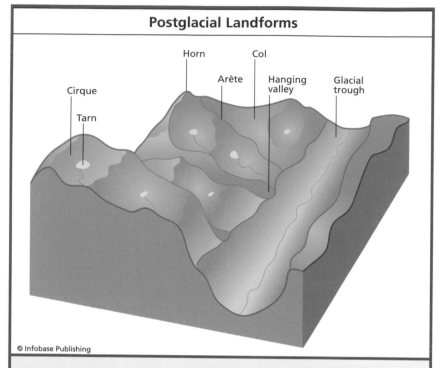

Horn   Col

Arête   Hanging   Glacial
valley   trough

Cirque

Tarn

© Infobase Publishing

Glaciers are large bodies of ice that move slowly down a slope or valley or spread outward on a land surface. This diagram illustrates some of the main glacial features, including horns, tarns, and cirques.

streams, hanging valleys are formed—valleys suspended above the glacial valley floor. Waterfalls often plunge from hanging valleys into the glacial valley below. (Within the United States, an example of this feature is the spectacular Bridal Veil Falls, in Yosemite National Park.) In places, basins are scoured and water-filled, resulting in what looks like a "string-of-beads" chain of small tarns, or mountain lakes of glacial origin. As glaciers move, they pick up till, or eroded rock material. This till forms moraines along the flanks of the moving ice or, if two or more glaciers join, within the glacier itself. In places where mountain glaciers reach the sea, they scour trenches that form long, narrow, U-shaped valleys into which the sea invades.

These features are the spectacular fjords that in the Northern Hemisphere add so much to the natural beauty of coastal Greenland, Norway, and parts of Alaska and Canada.

Patterned Ground

On a much smaller scale, the polar realm is home to some of the world's strangest landform features—patterned ground. From the air or another high vantage point, much of the flat to gently rolling Arctic land surface appears to be covered with strange symmetrical forms. They can appear as strips, lobes, nets, circles, or polygons. In size, the features vary from a foot across to several hundred feet (1/3 meter to 100 meters) in diameter. Although several forces are involved in their formation, the action of permafrost and ice, rapidly changing day-to-night temperatures, and local terrain are most responsible. Basically, temperature changes cause surface material to expand and contract. This, in turn, results in the natural sorting of rock materials by size and the deposition of different-sized materials in symmetrical shapes. Another feature unique to the region is the pingo, a rounded hill that can grow to a height of 200 feet (60 meters) above the surrounding flat terrain. A pingo can take thousands of years to form. The features are created by an ice core that grows from the bottom of a former lake, gradually thrusting upward through the overlying earth material.

PLANT AND ANIMAL LIFE

Most plants and animals thrive in hot, moist environments. For this reason, perhaps 80 percent or more of Earth's flora and fauna inhabit humid tropical lands. The distribution of plant and animal life can be illustrated by a pyramid with its broad base at the equator and peak at the North Pole. As plants and animals "climb" the pyramid, their survival becomes increasingly difficult. They encounter environmental barriers, such as cold, short periods of winter sunlight, aridity, permafrost, and other limiting factors.

Think of the environment as a series of sieves. Where it is warm and moist, the sieve has very large mesh, allowing millions of life-forms to pass through easily. The farther up the pyramid they move (that is, poleward from the tropical world), the mesh becomes smaller and smaller. By the time the Polar World is reached, the mesh is very fine. Only the hardiest life-forms can pass through and survive in the rigorous polar environment. Those that do are in some way uniquely adapted to the harsh conditions imposed by nature. As you would expect, of all the world's large ecosystems, the Polar World has the fewest number of species.

Flora

Most of the Polar World falls within the tundra ecosystem. *Tundra* is a Finnish word meaning "treeless plain" or "barren land." Both descriptions are quite appropriate in describing the region. For midlatitude people accustomed to the vertical landscape created by woodlands, the Arctic assumes a rather ominous horizontal dimension. Flat, featureless lands, often buried beneath a white cover of ice and snow, can easily disorient the traveler. Depth perception becomes difficult. Distances are all but impossible to measure visually in the absence of trees or other landmarks.

In locations experiencing perpetual ice cover, only a few hardy lichens and algae can survive. In some spots where algae thrive, their coloration creates a condition called "pink snow." Where the warmer temperatures of summer allow the surface to thaw even for a brief period, tundra vegetation springs to life. In order to survive, however, many environmental handicaps must be overcome. The growing season is very short and cool, and water remains in the frozen state much of the year. Due to windchill—which affects plants as well as humans—even above-freezing temperatures can plunge to subfreezing, killing conditions. Soils, where they exist, are very poor, thin, and nitrogen-deficient, and are often moisture saturated. Permafrost limits the depth to which roots can penetrate.

As was illustrated by the sieve analogy, plants do not arrive and then adapt to the Arctic's harsh environmental conditions. Rather, they have undergone a rigorous "survival of the fittest" challenge by passing through the series of environmental "sieves" with mesh of ever-decreasing sizes. In other words, plants (and animals as well) possessed traits that made their survival under harsh conditions possible *before* they reached the Arctic.

Different plants, of course, have different means of surviving. Most Arctic plants are small in size and low in stature. Hugging the ground, they take advantage of surface heat and also are less vulnerable to the wind's chilling effect. Some have small, leathery leaves, or hair-like growth on leaves and stems that offer some protection from the cold. Many flowering plants are annuals that burst into life as soon as the surface begins to thaw and go from seed to seed during a very short life cycle. As temperatures begin to warm, a carpet of green will appear. Several weeks later, the carpet will have turned into a spectacular carpet of blossoms. In a matter of weeks, however, all evidence of their life cycle will be gone. Seeds can last for many years, until conditions are right for once again sprouting to life. In fact, seeds estimated to be more than 10,000 years old germinated immediately when the silt in which they had been locked away thawed! Most plants are perennials, struggling from year to year, in order to survive, grow, and reproduce. Some woody plants (stunted trees) may be 100 years old, but have only grown several inches in size.

Despite the region's rather meager diversity of flora, there are about 250 species of mosses, 330 varieties of lichens, and an estimated 800 flowering plants in the North American Arctic alone. One plant is unique, being the only one capable of surviving in each of the world's ecosystems (except, of course, the ice cap). Can you guess what this hardy common yard pest is? The dandelion! There are also native grasses, low shrubs, and a few very small and scraggly trees, such as birch and willow, that grow in warmer, protected spots.

South of the tundra stretches the world's largest continuous woodland ecosystem, the vast taiga (or boreal forest) of North America and Eurasia. Most of the taiga lies to the south of the Polar World, but the region is important to some Arctic peoples. Needleleaf coniferous evergreen trees, such as pines, hemlock, spruce, and fir predominate in the North American taiga. Waxy needles offer some protection against the cold. The trees' dark color helps them absorb sunlight for warmth and also for photosynthesis, essential to plant growth. In Siberia, deciduous birches and larches (a needleleaf tree that loses its leaves each fall) are also common.

Trees in the taiga are generally quite small, with thin trunks, making them of little economic value other than for pulp and paper. They also grow closer together than do trees in most forests. Growing in dense stands helps protect the trees from chilling winds, but it also makes the taiga more vulnerable to earth-scorching forest fires. Unchecked, fires often rage for hundreds of miles, consuming everything in their devastating path. Even fires can have a positive effect, however. They tend to create open environments into which sunlight can fall. Here, the secondary growth consists of plants that are ideal for grazing and browsing animals.

Polar World cultures living in the tundra region are well adapted to treeless conditions. Along the many rivers that flow from the taiga forest northward through the tundra on their way to the Arctic, driftwood becomes available. Throughout most of the tundra, however, it is scarce, highly prized, and too valuable to be burned as fuel. Uses include frames for houses, tents, containers, boats, and sleds. It is also used for tools, weapons, snow knives (for making igloos), and other small items. Because of the lack of wood, animals play a vital role in sustaining native cultures.

Fauna

For many native peoples of the Polar World, the region's abundant fauna is the most important natural resource. Land animals, marine life, and birds provide the means for food, shelter, fuel, clothing, tools, and weapons. Their importance is recognized by the key position they hold in several native religions. Fauna also are the most important contributors to many folk (traditional) and contemporary (market) economies. In this section, the emphasis is placed on animal life as an element of the natural environment. The importance of animal life to humans is discussed in some detail in the following chapter.

Most Arctic animals are herbivorous (plant eaters). Of the herbivores, caribou and reindeer are far and away the most important. Even though they are closely related, they are also significantly different—North American caribou are wild, whereas Eurasian reindeer are domesticated. In fact, some people ride (domesticated) reindeer to hunt (wild) caribou! Both animals are amazingly well adapted to the Arctic environment. In addition to an extremely dense outer coat, they have a thick layer of fat, which protects them against the cold. Relative to body size, their hooves are among the largest of any animal. They function much like snowshoes, helping the animals easily cross snow- and ice-covered surfaces. The hooves' hard edges act as blades for digging beneath snow and ice for lichens and mosses.

Other important herbivores include the musk ox, polar hare, and lemming. Musk oxen are huge, horned, and buffalo-like in appearance. A full-grown bull may weigh up to 1,800 pounds (815 kilograms). Despite their name, the animals are neither oxen nor do they produce musk. These docile giants have long been valued for their meat, wool, and hides. Because of their economic importance and the fact that they possess no fear of humans, musk oxen were at one time nearly extinct. Today, their numbers are slowly increasing. Large herds are found on Ellesmere and other islands in the Canadian Archipelago, and in both Alaska and Greenland. Extensive research has been conducted on musk oxen at the University of Alaska in Fairbanks, and, in fact, the university has made considerable progress in domesticating the animal. If they are

A herd of caribou, or *tuktu*, as they are called by the Inuit, travel across the tundra in the Opingivik area of Canada's Baffin Island. Caribou are well adapted to the Arctic's frigid climate: They have a dense outer coat and a thick layer of fat to keep them warm.

successful, the musk ox would be the only new animal to be domesticated in more than 2,000 years!

The polar hare is hunted primarily for its heavy fur coat, which is used in making warm clothing. Lemmings, large ratlike animals, are important primarily as a source of food for carnivores. They are best known for suicidal marches to the sea when their numbers grow beyond the environment's ability to provide for their survival needs. Many other herbivorous animals, including moose, deer, and elk, inhabit the taiga forest region.

Life in the Arctic is a constant "survival of the fittest." Herbivores eat vegetation, carnivores eat herbivores, and humans are the enemy of both. In addition, cloud-like swarms of flies, mosquitoes, and gnats feast upon and make life miserable for all other life-forms! Wolves, foxes, wolverines, coyotes, and weasels are among the Arctic's more common carnivorous wildlife. Moving southward to the taiga, bears, including the huge grizzly, become commonplace.

Perhaps the best-known animal of the Arctic is the polar bear, which, like humans, is omnivorous—it eats both animal and plant life. Unlike other bears, the polar bear does not hibernate, although females will dig a snow cave when they are about to give birth. Unknowingly walking over and falling through the roof of a snow cave into the den of a female bear and her cubs is a terrifying (and perhaps fatal) experience! Bears have a varied diet but feed primarily on seals that

Reindeer and Caribou
All-purpose Animals

Native peoples of the Polar World use nearly all parts of a reindeer or caribou; nothing goes to waste. The animal's flesh is the primary source of food for both people and their dogs. Fat is also consumed by humans. To an Eskimo child, eyeballs are a delicacy much as hard candy is to children from the midlatitudes. Even the rumen, or stomach contents, is consumed. The partially digested reindeer moss, lichens, and other plants provide the only vegetable material that is otherwise lacking in the diet of many native people.

Fat is also used for fuel. Skins are used to make clothing, summer tents, wall coverings, and the shell of kayaks and other watercraft. The gut is used to make raincoats and window panes, and to waterproof boots. Tools and weapons are made from bone and antlers, and bone marrow is considered a delicacy by many people. Teeth are used as ornaments. Finally, domesticated reindeer are used in much the same way as are animal domesticates in the lower latitudes—for milking, riding, and pulling sleds.

they catch and kill on or near sea ice. Scientists are deeply concerned about the polar bears' future. At Churchill, on the western coast of Canada's Hudson Bay, ice that is essential to their hunting is disappearing three to four weeks earlier than it did several decades ago. Here, the bear population is declining, and their average weight has dropped by about 15 percent.

Sea life is exceptionally rich in the Polar World. Seals, walrus, and otters have long been prized for their pelts. The seal, in particular, has been the "staple" for many Arctic peoples. In a traditional culture, each individual typically would need about 25 to 30 seals a year. As is the case with caribou and reindeer, every bit of the animal is used; none of it goes to waste. Walruses have been prized for their ivory tusks (now protected) and their fat, which makes excellent blubber for burning. Sea otters have excellent pelts, once valued at up to $1,000 each. By the early twentieth century, however, they were nearly extinct. Today, under protection, their numbers are increasing in some locations.

Whales have long been a mainstay of coastal peoples, particularly the gigantic arctic blue. These aquatic giants are the world's largest living animal. They can grow to 120 feet (36 meters) in length and weigh nearly 225 tons (30 times greater than the largest elephants). No wonder a single whale could feed and fuel an entire village for a full year! Today, many whales, including the arctic blue, are endangered species. Waters of the Polar World teem with fish that provide a dietary staple for many coastal- and riverside-dwelling peoples. Fish are eaten fresh (and raw), or preserved by smoking, drying, or salting.

Hundreds of bird species flock (literally) to the Arctic. Some remain there throughout the year, but many others are migratory, traveling from as far south as southern Argentina. Each spring, countless millions of ducks and geese from mid-latitude locations—including an estimated 40 percent of all North American waterfowl—migrate to breeding grounds in the Arctic. In the autumn, flying in their distinctive V-shaped flocks, they return southward. The strange-looking ptarmigan (with feathers on the soles of its feet!) is perhaps the most important bird for the Arctic's inhabitants. Its range is the entire Arctic region, where its flesh and eggs are eaten and its soft skin is used in sewing garments.

One of the most lasting memories of anyone visiting the polar realm during summer months will certainly be the hordes of insects. Huge swarms of ravenous, blood-sucking mosquitoes, gnawing gnats, and ferocious biting flies make life absolutely miserable for man and beast alike throughout much of the region. David Berreby, writing in *Discover*, described a "swat test," in which dead mosquitoes are counted after a flat-handed swat of some part of the body. His record was an incredible 270!

WATER FEATURES

About 90 percent of all the world's lakes occupy basins scoured by glacial action. It is little wonder that the Polar World has more lakes than the rest of the world combined. It is also home to some of the world's largest rivers—and, yes, contrary to a common myth, many rivers, including most in the Arctic region, *do* flow northward!

If one views them from the air during summer months, it is apparent that lakes dominate much of the Arctic land-scape. Some of these freshwater bodies occupy deep basins. These "great" lakes include Canada's Great Bear, Great Slave, Athabasca, and Winnipeg, as well as many of the larger lakes of Eurasia. Most of these water features, however (hundreds of thousands of them), are small and shallow. Known as "thaw" lakes, they occupy slight depressions filled by meltwater from the active layer of frozen ground, as well as ice and melted snow.

In most locations, the depressions occupied by these bodies of water would be dry. In the Arctic, however, several conditions combine to retain surface water. First, because permafrost lies just below the surface, water does not sink deeply into the ground. Second, stream patterns were deranged by the glaciers that once blanketed the region. As a result, most streams are poorly developed and unable to adequately drain the surface. They flow very short distances, often only from pond to pond. Third, much of the land is extremely flat, further hindering runoff. This is true even in those areas where mature streams flow through to the Arctic Ocean or some other large water body. Finally, because of low temperatures, very little surface moisture is evaporated.

Just as it has many lakes, the Polar World also has more rivers than perhaps anyplace except the humid tropics. Most of them, as explained earlier, are short. The region does have some huge streams, however. Many Arctic rivers flow from south to north, from the wetter taiga across the arid tundra and into the Arctic Ocean. In North America, the largest is Canada's mighty Mackenzie, which in volume ranks among the continent's greatest rivers. To the west, the Yukon River wanders across Alaska before entering the Bering Sea. Three of the world's 10 largest rivers (by volume) flow northward across Siberia and into the Arctic. The Ob and Yenisey rivers drain the swampy Western Siberian Lowland. Further to the east, in Yakutia, the Lena flows northward from near Russia's border with China, through the world's coldest inhabited region.

Because of their location, the region's rivers are of limited value for hydroelectric development or navigation. They pose other problems, as well. Flowing from south to north, their headwaters thaw months before ice and snow melts in the lower (northern) stream course. As a result, when northward-flowing water meets the frozen river channel, there is no place for it go other than to jump the stream's banks. Vast areas are flooded annually. Fortunately, little damage results from the floodwaters, because there is so little human settlement. Because they flow into the Arctic Ocean, the streams are of minimal value to navigation, although some local river traffic does occur. Both hydroelectric potential and navigation are further hindered by another factor: Because moisture in their drainage basins is frozen much of the year, up to 90 percent of the runoff takes place during a two- to three-month period. Finally, because the south-to-north-flowing streams are very wide and subject to flooding, they impose a major barrier to east-west surface travel.

There are many problems related to water in the Arctic. Perhaps you have heard the old cliché: "Water, water everywhere, but not a drop to drink." (This is actually a line from the poem "The Rime of the Ancient Mariner," by Samuel Taylor Coleridge, written in 1797.) For many months, this is true of the Polar World, where water seems to be everywhere, but in the form of ice and snow. During the long winter, obtaining water is a major problem. Groundwater is locked in permafrost. Unprotected pipes can freeze. In many locations, there is little snow to melt, and even where it is, fuel may be scarce. The human water intake requirement (about 5.5 pints or 2.6 liters per day), however, is about the same in the Arctic as it is in the midlatitudes. Traditionally, ice or snow must be melted to provide water for human and animal consumption. In addition, water in the liquid state must be kept from (re)freezing. Needless to say, bathing is a rare event for most Arctic natives!

To this point, the book has emphasized the physical aspects of the polar environment. Our attention now turns to the human, or cultural aspects of the region's geographic conditions and patterns. In the next chapter, you will learn about ancient peoples, traditional cultures, and recent migrants to the region. Emphasis will focus on how different peoples have met the environmental challenges and taken advantage of the opportunities the region offers. First, we will consider those people who have made this seemingly hostile region their home for thousands of years—native peoples of the Polar World.

5

Native Peoples

Nowhere else on Earth have native peoples adapted to a more inhospitable and challenging natural environment than in the Polar World. Here, nature imposes seemingly insurmountable obstacles to economic survival, mobility, and comfort. And nature can also be deadly. Below freezing temperatures are uncompromising; they make finding a suitable shelter an important task. Humans are biologically adapted to a tropical climate. Our bodies begin to feel the effects of cold at about 77°F (25°C) and must be protected. It is not our bodies that allow us to live in the Arctic; rather, it is culture that is humankind's "adaptive mechanism."

Any humans who survive today or in times past in environments beyond the tropics have done so because of their culture. Their way of life—including their knowledge, tools, skills, clothing, housing, and other survival strategies—has made survival possible. People inhabiting Arctic environments had to be culturally adapted

From the time they first arrived in the Siberian Arctic 35,000 years ago, native people have adapted to the region's harsh conditions. For millennia, Inuit people, such as this man, have been building igloos to serve as shelters in an environment devoid of any other building material.

to conditions of severe cold *before* they occupied the region. Remarkably, there is evidence that they were able to do so at least 35,000 years ago, if not earlier. This chapter focuses primarily on the traditional ways of life practiced by Polar World peoples. In this context, it is important to remember that today, for most native cultures, their traditional lifestyle is little more than a distant memory.

THE ICE AGE AND EARLY HUMANS

Archaeological evidence from Europe suggests that humans lived at the margins of ice age glaciers tens if not hundreds of thousands of years ago. This suggests that they had control of fire, adequate protective clothing and footwear, suitable housing, and a means of subsistence that was well adapted to extreme cold. Recently, archaeologists discovered some startling evidence near the mouth of the Yana River in eastern Siberia. Here, hugging the frigid Arctic coast, human artifacts were found and dated to some 35,000 years ago. This, of course, comes as a great shock to anyone inclined to think of early humans as being "primitive." "Knowledge," it can be said, is "learning for living." These peoples were living on the fringe of the inhabitable world; in what is today Earth's coldest inhabited region. In order to survive, they had to have a keen understanding of the environment and its resources. They also had to possess knowledge and skills that made their survival possible under conditions of severe cold.

OLD WORLD–NEW WORLD EXCHANGES

As you learned in Chapter 3, during the ice age, global sea level was an estimated 400 to 450 feet (120 to 140 meters) lower than it is today. As ocean levels dropped, a corridor of land 1,300 miles (2,100 kilometers) wide—today the floor of the Bering Sea—joined Asia and North America. This span of then-dry land formed what scientists call the Bering Strait Land Bridge, or Beringia. This was the route taken by many animals migrating between Eurasia and the Americas. Many scientists also believe it was the route taken by early humans migrating to the Americas.

It is certain that the first people to occupy the Americas came from elsewhere. Decades ago, archaeologists and other scientists thought they knew who these early people were and where they came from. They also believed that they knew how and by what route they traveled to their new homeland and even when they arrived. It was believed that Asian peoples, in pursuit of large game animals, crossed Beringia into present-day Alaska. Then, heading southward, they passed through a very narrow ice-free corridor, 1,200 to 1,500 miles (1,900 to 2,400 kilometers) in length, located between two huge masses of glacial ice that then covered much of northern North

America. Finally, they supposedly reached the southwestern United States some 10,000 to 15,000 years ago.

Now, many archaeologists, geographers, and others are shaking their heads in bewilderment. As more and more evidence is gathered, the origin of the earliest Americans has become a gigantic question mark. In fact, it ranks as one of the great unanswered social science mysteries of our time. Some archaeological finds suggest, for example, that the earliest Americans may have come from various areas. Northeastern Siberia, of course, remains the primary source region, but points of origin in Southeast Asia, Japan, Australia, Europe, and even Africa also have been suggested!

In regard to the Beringia route and ice-free corridor theory, some scientists now suggest that this route would have been far too cold and inhospitable for human migration. Some even question the existence of the proposed (but never proved) ice-free corridor. Rather, they believe a coastal route may have been followed. With sea levels lowered, the broad continental shelf (land gradually sloping away from continental land-masses and now beneath water) was exposed. People simply could have walked between Asia and North America following the Pacific coast.

The coastal-route theory has much in its favor. Conditions would have been much warmer, with temperatures near or above freezing because of warm ocean currents (currents similar to today's Gulf Stream and North Atlantic Drift that bathe northwestern Europe with warm water). Food would have been plentiful from both land and sea. Ample supplies of driftwood would have been available for fuel, making tools and weapons, constructing shelters, and even building boats or rafts needed to get around glacial lobes that reached the sea. A few scientists even believe that at least some of the earliest Americans may have come by boat! (If this sounds far-fetched, you must remember that Australia was inhabited perhaps 50,000 years ago, requiring at least some travel across open sea.) Even when the first Americans arrived is now a hotly debated question.

Various "guesstimates" based on the scientific interpretation of evidence place the earliest arrivals at any time between 12,000 to 100,000 years ago!

Perhaps we will never know the full story of the earliest Americans. In fact, other than being of scientific interest, the answer really is unimportant. It is probable that some arrivals came by way of routes other than Beringia and were of several racial groups other than Asian Mongoloid peoples. What is quite certain is that the great majority of early American peoples did come from eastern Asia. And the route they took at least touched upon today's Polar World. This, of course, suggests that, from the very dawn of settlement, the new arrivals possessed survival strategies that made it possible to live in the Arctic.

Several things can be said with some certainty about the earliest Americans, including those of the Arctic region. When Europeans arrived on the shores of what to them was a New World, they reached a land that had been "discovered" and settled many thousands of years earlier. That population, it is widely believed, was dominantly East Asian in terms of physical characteristics and geographical origin. The ways of life practiced by the native peoples varied greatly in terms of language, economic activity, housing and dress, and many other aspects of culture. Levels of cultural attainment ranged from well-organized, high-level "civilizations," to small groups of isolated peoples who possessed a very meager level of material culture.

POLAR WORLD CULTURES

The Polar World is home to an estimated 200,000 to 250,000 native peoples. Although they had much in common, differences also existed in the traditional cultures practiced from place to place. Emphasis here focuses upon these traditional ways of living.

Confusion in Names

Polar World peoples recognize themselves by many names, both collectively and as individual (tribal) groups. In the

The Sami people are indigenous to northern areas of Sweden, Finland, and Norway, and the Lola Peninsula of Russia. They traditionally led nomadic lifestyles in which they engaged in such occupations as reindeer herding, hunting, fishing, and trapping, but today many Samis lead modern lives.

American Arctic, names such as "Eskimo" and "Indian," for example, are widely recognized and used. In Eurasia, "Lapps" and "Reindeer People" are common. These are not the names by which these people identified themselves, however. *Eskimo* is a corruption of the French word for "eaters of raw meat," and *Indian* is derived from one of the great geographical errors of all time—Columbus's belief that he had reached the East Indies. Today, many native cultures worldwide, including those in the Arctic, are returning to the use of their own original names, and this can be confusing.

In Alaska, *Eskimo* appears to be acceptable, although certainly not by all members of the ethnic group. In Canada, however, *Inuit* is preferred and in Greenland, *Kalaallit*. Throughout their realm, Eskimo peoples also are recognized by many local names. Indians, as a group, may be identified as Native Americans, First Americans, or First Nations (preferred in Canada). Individual tribes, too, often have several names. In northern Scandinavia, for example, the Lapps now prefer to be called Sami. The terms used throughout this book are those most widely recognized and also those used by the U.S. Census Bureau.

Unique Characteristics

Traditional Polar World cultures are unique in several very important ways. First, few of the world's peoples live in greater isolation. Several groups, when first contacted by outsiders, were shocked—they assumed that they were the only people on Earth! Second, isolation contributed to relative cultural uniformity. Very few new ideas or material traits reached Polar World peoples from other cultures until quite recently. Third, because of the lack of diffusion—the flow of outside ideas—native cultures had to be extremely innovative. They had to develop survival strategies that allowed them to live in the harsh Arctic environment. Finally, people of the realm identified and used a resource base much different than that of midlatitude peoples. Many resources that we take for granted—iron ore, coal, petroleum, and other minerals, for example—were not used at all. Conversely, the resources upon which these people depended, such as ice, snow, driftwood, and all parts of many animals, are not things upon which we depend for our survival.

Common to all traditional Polar World people is a great dependence on animal life. Animals provide food, clothing, shelter, tools, weapons, and mobility. The sledge, pulled by dogs in North America and reindeer in much of Eurasia, is used for travel throughout the region. Because they depend upon animals (hunted in North America and both herded and hunted in Eurasia), most cultures are nomadic. Rather than wandering aimlessly, nomads follow well-established routes on a seasonal basis. Because they move frequently, shelters are generally crude and temporary. They may be made of earth, stone, wood (where available), animal hides, snow, or a combination of materials. As is true of other nomadic peoples, material possessions are few. Socially and economically, many groups practice a form of communal living. People take care of one another and if someone is in need, help is never far away. Everyone is pretty much alike in terms of "wealth." There are no "rich" and "poor" in traditional Polar World societies. In most instances, even leadership is fluid. A skilled hunter will be looked to for leadership during a hunt and a skilled builder may be called upon to direct the building of a new settlement.

Despite the many similarities in Polar World cultures, there also are some sharp differences. Geographically, the primary division is between the North American and Eurasian peoples. Although they occupy quite similar natural environments, the way the respective groups use their land and resources varies greatly. Eskimo (Inuit) and Aleut peoples depend primarily on marine life, whales, sea mammals, and fish. Hence, their settlements tend to cling to coastal areas. In Eurasia, on the other hand, people are reindeer herders and hunters of land animals. Their economic base and settlements are most often found inland, including in the northern taiga.

North American Polar Peoples

The North American Arctic is home to a number of different cultures; the best known is the Eskimo (Inuit). Others include the Aleut and Indians. Some 8,000 Aleuts, a hunting, fishing, and gathering people, live in settlements scattered across the 1,100-mile (1,800-kilometer) chain of Aleutian Islands. Athabaskan Indians occupy portions of northern Alaska and northwestern and north-central Canada. These First Tribes people share ancient linguistic roots but are now divided into many subgroups, such as the Gwich'in. These people live inland, on the southern margin of the tundra and in the taiga forest. They depend primarily on hunting caribou for their livelihood. The Eskimo are far and away the most numerous, widely distributed, and best known of the North American Arctic native peoples.

The Eskimo

Eskimo, or Inuit, culture is recognized by its relatively uniform language, dependence on marine resources, and coastal residence. One must use caution, however, in stereotyping an "Eskimo." The image that no doubt comes to mind is of a person living in a snow igloo, wearing a fur-fringed parka, and traveling by kayak or dog sled. He is an avid and skilled hunter who uses a harpoon to catch seals, whales, and other mammals. Great pleasure is derived from eating blubber (could this be the origin of our slang expression "chewing the fat" for social conversation?) and raw meat. This composite Eskimo, however, never existed. These images are a collection of traits taken from throughout the Eskimo realm. Most Eskimos, for example, never built or even saw an igloo!

In terms of their range and settlement, Eskimos are somewhat unique among the world's native cultures. They occupied an area greater than that of any other New World aboriginal (first) peoples and in areal extent, they were exceeded only by the Polynesian peoples of the Pacific Basin. Their territory extends from the eastern tip of Siberia to eastern Greenland— one-third the distance around the world! Eskimo villages in northern Greenland are the world's most northerly permanent habitations. Southward, their settlements also are scattered along the Labrador coast. Yet within this vast expanse, the total area actually occupied is quite small. You will recall that much of the interior is relatively inhospitable because of surface water, swamps and marshes, insects, and other limiting factors. Most settlements, therefore, are along the coast, leaving much of the interior vacant.

In many respects, Eskimos were inventive geniuses. Few if any traditional cultures can match their innovative skills. The snow igloo is an architectural marvel based on the principle of the vaulted dome. Imagine taking snow to build a structure that is warm, comfortable, durable, and relatively easy to construct! Much of our warm, lightweight, comfortable winter wear—including headgear, clothing, gloves, and footwear—was copied directly from what the Eskimos have made and worn for millennia. Their secret was to use two layers of material separated by duck down, thereby allowing air to serve as insulation against the cold. The sturdy Eskimo kayak has become a popular recreational and sport watercraft, and the effectiveness of their dog-pulled sleds is illustrated each year in Alaska's Iditarod Trail Sled Dog Race from Anchorage to Nome (see sidebar on the next page). Many polar explorers were successful only after they adopted Eskimo cultural practices, including use of dog sleds, clothing, diet, and other traits.

The Eskimo diet consists almost entirely of raw meat and fat. Nutritionists are amazed that such a diet can be so healthy. Eskimo hunting strategies rank among the world's most effective. Their harpoon, used in hunting walruses, seals, and small whales, has been called the world's finest aboriginal weapon. It consists of a detachable spear and shaft, both of which are linked by long leather "ropes" to inflated animal bladders. When the harpoon becomes imbedded in the animal, it separates from the shaft. The float not only tires the struggling and weakened animal but also keeps it from going under water. Whereas marine life is the Eskimo mainstay, some groups do occasionally venture inland to hunt caribou. With such extremes between summer and winter, it is not surprising that Eskimo society and culture are in tune to seasonal changes. The amount of light, surface conditions, and the availability of game are all factors that influence their activities.

During the cold, dark winter, most Eskimos can be found in small coastal settlements. Winter is the preferred season. It is a time of eating, sleeping, and socializing. Travel is easy across the frozen surface, and the hordes of summer insects are but a distant memory. The arrival of spring, despite its environmental problems, is greatly anticipated. At that point, food supplies are becoming scarce, and various forms of marine life (walruses, seals, and whales) begin to appear in the cracks of open water that now can be seen between slabs of retreating sea ice. Migratory birds arrive, and their eggs are a delicacy that breaks the monotony of a diet based on raw

Alaska's Iditarod
The "Last Great Race on Earth"

Imagine traveling 1,150 (average) miles (1,850 kilometers)—the distance between Orlando, Florida, and Chicago, Illinois—with a sled pulled by 12 to 16 dogs. Depending on conditions, you must make the trip in as little as 9 or 10 days. Your journey takes you across some of the world's most difficult terrain. Between Anchorage and your destination in Nome, you will pass through dense taiga forests, cross rugged mountain passes, and pick your way through the wooden skeletons of burned forest. Eventually, you reach the desolate tundra. Along your route are a few small native villages. Temperatures during the trip may drop far below zero. Howling winds add to your misery, with their chilling effect and blinding blizzards. Much of your trip is made in darkness. Your body and mind are numb from lack of sleep. No wonder the Iditarod is called the "Last Great Race on Earth"!

In addition to being the world's most grueling competitive event, it is unique in another way: Women and men compete on even terms, and women have won on a number of occasions. The mushers come from all walks of life. There are doctors and lawyers, as well as loggers, miners, and fishermen. The youngest person to participate was 18 and the oldest 86. Whether male or female, young or old, winner or loser, the race pits mushers and their dog teams against nature's worst and Alaska's best. It is a wonderful tribute to the endurance of meat and fat. This is a time for gathering driftwood. Men will often travel inland to hunt musk ox and caribou. Later, as autumn's chill and darkness descend upon the land, people once again settle in for the long winter. Their new village may be many miles removed from the previous winter's site. Only

humans and their faithful dogs and to the competitive human spirit. For more information on the Iditarod, see the official Web site: *http://www.iditarod.com*

The Iditarod Trail Sled Dog Race is held each year in March and is billed as the "Last Great Race." The race, which starts in Anchorage and ends up in Nome, Alaska, covers 1,150 miles and competitors cross mountains, forest, tundra, and frozen rivers in hopes of claiming a piece of the $750,000 prize. Pictured here is Bill Pinkham of Colorado leading his team of dogs during the 2005 Iditarod.

recently have the Eskimo begun living in permanently settled communities.

EURASIAN PEOPLES

Native peoples of the Eurasian Arctic are rather loosely organized into numerous tribes that speak diverse languages. Essentially, they are unified by two factors: dependence on reindeer and avoidance of the coastal region. Most groups migrate seasonally between the taiga forest and the treeless tundra. Among the better-known groups, from west to east, are the Sami (Lapps) of northern Scandinavia and adjacent areas of Russia; Nenet (Samoyed) of northern Europe and Russia; Evenk (Tungus), Yakut (Sakha) and Yukaghir (Odul) of northern Siberia; and the Chukchi, who occupy far eastern Siberia, across the Bering Strait from Alaska. Because of racial and ethnic mixing, it is difficult to know how many native peoples remain in Eurasia today. What is known is that the number is very small, and they occupy a huge, desolate, and frigid land. Population densities are among the lowest in the world.

For all these peoples, traditional culture revolved around the reindeer. These animals were first domesticated from the wild caribou of northern Eurasia several thousand years ago. The idea of domestication and use of domesticated animals is believed to have diffused northward from horse and cattle breeders and herders of Central Asia. In the west, the Samis have fully domesticated and tamed the reindeer. The animal provides milk and meat. It is used to pull sleds and also serves as a pack animal. It is even ridden by humans.

Reindeer have a considerable advantage over dogs. They can graze, whereas dogs must be fed; they can travel over more rugged surfaces and in worse weather; and in an emergency, part of the team can be eaten! A full-grown reindeer can carry up to about 150 pounds (68 kilograms) and cover a distance of 50 miles (80 kilometers) in one day. In north-central Asia, the reindeer is domesticated but is used only to pull sleds and as a source of meat. Eastern tribes have not fully utilized the animals. Here, reindeer are semiwild and only hunted as much as are the caribou of the American Arctic.

Reindeer migrate, often hundreds of miles, and most Asian Arctic peoples follow these migrations. The winter months find them in the sheltered environment of the taiga forest. These peoples' shelter, often a tent or crude pit house dug into the earth and covered with animal skins, may seem ill-suited to the region's frigid temperatures. In the taiga, though, they have ample wood for fuel, as well as for building and carving. During the spring and summer, the herds migrate northward onto the open plains of the tundra. They are followed, of course, by hunters. Late in the summer, roots, tubers, and berries can be gathered—a welcome change to a nearly all-meat diet.

The ways of living described in this chapter are but a distant memory to most Polar World cultures. Midlatitude peoples began arriving in their remote homelands at various times in history and for a variety of reasons. Some native peoples have all but given up their traditional culture. Others cling to a way of life that they fear will be lost forever if the ways of midlatitude people are adopted. Today, this clash between past and present results in a collision between traditional and modern values and lifestyles that reverberates throughout the polar realm. In the following chapter, the arrival of midlatitude peoples is highlighted.

6

European Influences

With but few exceptions, the Polar World was a "last frontier" for exploration, settlement, and exploitation by people of European culture. Even today, most of the region lacks a significant European presence, as indicated by population, landscape, or cultural imprint. In fact, much of the region has never been seen (from the surface) by nonnative eyes. Most contact between natives and outsiders has been during the past century. Because of these encounters, however, many native cultures are undergoing rapid— and often extremely painful—changes.

Europeans have come to the Arctic for many reasons. The first were the fearless explorers who ventured northward into cold, uncharted lands. They were followed by fishermen, trappers, missionaries, and traders. Miners were attracted by the lure of mineral wealth in some areas. Finally, scientists, adventurers, government officials (including military), and a few permanent settlers were drawn to the remote and frigid Arctic region. This chapter discusses the history, nature, and consequences of European influence within the Polar World. (In this and subsequent chapters, "European" refers to nonnative Polar World peoples of European culture, including Canadians and Americans.)

EUROPEAN CONTACTS
Pytheas of Massilia (c. 325 B.C.)

No one knows for sure who the first Europeans to reach the Polar World were or, for that matter, when or where the earliest contact occurred. The first documented account of European travel to the Arctic region, however, is that of a Greek venturer, Pytheas of Massilia. In about 325 B.C., Pytheas traveled northward, to a land he called "Thule." Historical geographers are uncertain of the exact route he took, or the location of Thule. He described a place six sailing days north of Britain that was located one sailing day from the "frozen sea." The area was described as being neither land, nor sea, nor air, but a blend of them, like a "sea lung" in which land and sea floated. He reported that north of Thule, there was no darkness during the summer months and no light during the winter.

Many Greeks (and later historians) doubted Pytheas's claims. Mediterranean peoples, after all, were totally unfamiliar with Arctic conditions. The very they most questioned, though, are those that now lend support to his account. Certainly, his description of conditions in which land, sea, and air blend together is very typical of fogbound, snow- and ice-covered northern land and water surfaces. Anyone who has ever seen surf rolling beneath a water surface of floating pieces of ice can easily identify the source of the sea lung. As the ice-covered water surface rises and falls with each passing wave, it gives the appearance of "breathing." And Pytheas's account of the summer sunlight and winter darkness certainly describes conditions in the far north. Many scholars now believe that Pytheas's travels took him to coastal Norway, in the vicinity of the Arctic Circle. Although the exact location of Pytheas's Thule remains shrouded in mystery, the name lives on. Thule Air Force Base in northwestern Greenland, a U.S. military installation, is home to the world's largest satellite tracking facility.

Vikings (Ninth to Eleventh Centuries)

The next documented European explorers and settlers in the Polar World were the Vikings from Scandinavia. These brave

Did a Bull Change History?

According to Viking sagas (stories), a group of about 160 Viking men and women from the Greenland settlement arrived in Vineland (what is probably now Newfoundland) during the summer of 1003. Here, under the leadership of Thorfinn Karlsefni, they founded a small settlement they named Hop. The Norse were quite happy to escape the cold, barren, desolate coasts of Greenland and settle in a land teeming with wildlife, timber, and freshwater. According to the sagas, they intended to create a permanent settlement that would eventually grow into a larger colony in this new land that offered such great abundance. With permanence in mind, they even brought livestock—including a bull owned by Karlsefni. And here unfolds one of history's strangest events!

Soon after their arrival, the Vikings began trading with a group of people they called Scraelings. The relationship went well until one day Karlsefni's bull suddenly charged from the forest. The Scraelings, who of course had never seen cattle, were terrified of this huge, strange, enraged beast and fled in terror. Soon thereafter, they returned and attacked the Viking village. Several Norse were killed and a number of others were injured. The Norse, realizing that they were outnumbered and would never be safe in Vineland, decided to abandon Hop and return to Greenland. Thus ended the Vikings' attempt to permanently settle in North America. Did Karlsefni's enraged bull delay the permanent European settlement of the Americas for and skilled voyagers reached and settled Iceland by A.D. 874. By 984, under the leadership of Eric the Red, they reached Greenland. His naming of the huge island suggests that Eric was quite a con artist. Iceland, after all, is mainly green, whereas most of Greenland is buried beneath ice. By naming the island Greenland, Eric hoped to attract Norse settlers from

some 500 years? How different might the historical and cultural geography of northern North America be had it not been for Karlsefni's bull?

L'Anse aux Meadows, which is today a National Historic Park, is the only preserved Viking settlement in North America. Located on the northern tip of Newfoundland, the settlement was discovered by Norwegian explorer Dr. Helge Ingstad and his archaeologist wife, Dr. Anne Stine Ingstad, in 1960.

Iceland. Although Scandinavians disappeared from Greenland by the thirteenth century, the island remains politically tied to Denmark.

By around 1000, Vikings sailing westward from Greenland reached a place they named Helluland (Rocky Land), an apt description of the eastern coast of Baffin Island. A few days of sailing southward brought them to Markland (Forest Land), no doubt the coast of Labrador. Finally, they reached Vineland the Good. For years, the location of Vineland was mere speculation; in fact, most historians doubted that such a place actually was reached by the Vikings. During the mid-twentieth century, however, a Viking village was discovered and excavated. Today, tourists can visit the reconstructed settlement at L'Anse aux Meadows, a National Historic Park on the northern tip of Canada's Newfoundland.

Russian Cossacks (Seventeenth to Nineteenth Centuries)

By 1581, Cossacks—fiercely independent peoples of Eastern Europe—had crossed the Ural Mountains and conquered the Kingdom of Sibir. Thus began a period of territorial expansion from Moscow that within 70 years spanned Siberia and ultimately reached far into North America. As was to happen decades later in the North American Arctic, the chief attraction was fur-bearing animals, particularly the Siberian sable (marten). During their expansion, the Cossacks explored, charted new lands, contacted and interacted with Polar World peoples, and even settled some areas. By 1650, they had reached the Bering Strait and continued on into North America.

During the first half of the eighteenth century, Russian explorers lay claim to what is now Alaska. (By 1812, they had pushed as far south as Fort Ross, a Russian outpost located on the California coast about 100 miles [160 kilometers] north of San Francisco.) In 1867, the United States purchased Alaska from Russia. The sale price for 586,412 square miles (1,518,800 square kilometers) was $7.2 million. At the time, the public was outraged over such expenditure for a remote "polar icebox." The purchase was dubbed "Seward's Folly." (William Seward was the U.S. secretary of state who engineered the purchase.) Today, however, the state of Alaska contributes more to the U.S. economy *daily* than its purchase price! Also, can you imagine how different the outcome of the cold war might have been had Alaska remained in the hands of the Soviet Union?

LOOKING FOR A ROUTE TO THE FAR EAST

The Polar World is one of the few remaining places on Earth to which explorers are still attracted. Portions of Siberia and large areas of Antarctica remain largely unseen and uncharted (from the ground). Surprisingly, perhaps, the wealth of the tropical Far East, particularly the East Indies and their treasured spices, played a key role in Arctic exploration! When Columbus sailed west to reach the east, he and many explorers who followed encountered a huge barrier lying in their way—the Americas. For several centuries, much of the exploration conducted in the New World was motivated by an attempt to find a water route through or around the Americas. Historical accounts of polar exploration make for wonderful reading. Unfortunately, space does not allow a detailed account of the many courageous souls who braved the elements (and often died) in their attempt to unlock the mysteries of the Arctic Ocean Basin.

The Northwest Passage

Most exploration for a water route around the Americas focused on the Northwest Passage—a route through the Canadian Archipelago and on to the Bering Strait. The incredibly difficult task confronting explorers is evident when looking at a map of the area lying between Greenland and Alaska. Add to the incredible maze of channels and island barriers the fact that nearly all of the Arctic was frozen most if not all of the year. In addition, summers are very short and it was not possible for sailing vessels to make the passage during a single season.

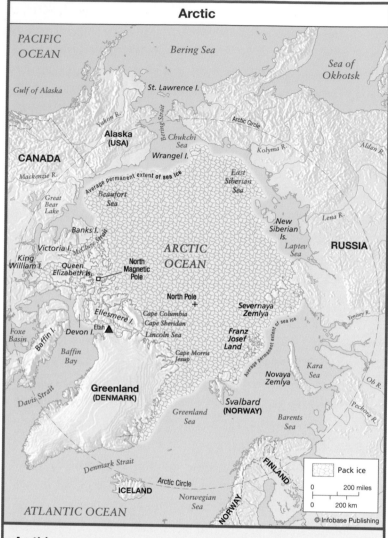

As this present-day map of the Arctic illustrates, explorers of the 1500 and 1600s were confronted with a difficult task in their search for a northwest passage to Asia. Discovering an all-season water route was nearly impossible, because much of the Arctic Ocean is frozen throughout the year.

The search for a northern water route between the Atlantic and Pacific oceans began in 1500, when Portuguese sailor Gaspar Corte Real ventured into North Atlantic waters. He sailed northward along both the east and west coasts of Greenland, perhaps reaching as far north as the Arctic Circle. Corte Real believed that he had reached the northeastern coast of Asia. Nearly 75 years would pass, however, before another navigator ventured into the treacherous waters west of Greenland. Between 1576 and 1578, British sailor Martin Frobisher explored the area of the Hudson Straight, the water passage between the Atlantic Ocean and Hudson Bay. Frobisher believed that he had discovered the long-sought passageway. He assumed that Asia was the land to his right and America that on his left. In 1585 and 1586, British sailor John Davis explored much of the sea that bears his name—that lying between Greenland and Baffin Island. His adventures took him as far north as 73 degrees, which, at the time, was the most northerly point yet reached by Europeans.

Henry Hudson is the best known of the early explorers who sought the increasingly elusive Northwest Passage. Hudson was British, but his 1608–1609 voyage in his ship, the *Half Moon*, was financially backed by the Netherlands. After exploring the area around the mouth of the Hudson River, he sailed northward. His tragic end is well documented. After reaching Baffin Island and turning west into the huge bay that now bears his name, his crew mutinied. They put Henry, his son, and a few sick or injured sailors in a small dingy and set them free in the bay to perish. No trace of Hudson was ever found.

The search for the elusive Northwest Passage would continue for two more centuries. With each new venture, it became increasingly apparent that no all-season water route existed. Amazingly, it was not until 1903–1906 that Norwegian Roald Amundsen and his ship, the *Göja*, finally navigated the passage. No American vessel made the crossing until 1950, when it was achieved by a Coast Guard icebreaker. Today, although the passage has been made on a number of occasions, the route is of little commercial use. The Trans-Alaska Pipeline was constructed because it was impractical to transport petroleum from Prudhoe Bay, through the Bering Strait, and into the Pacific Ocean.

In the 1600s, Englishman Henry Hudson was one of several explorers who failed in their attempts to find a northwest passage to Asia. On his third voyage, Hudson's crew mutinied and sent him, his son, and a few sick crew members adrift in a small boat. Hudson was never heard from again and a northwest passage was not discovered until the early 1900s.

Attempts to find and navigate a water route to Asia by way of a northeast passage proved to be equally elusive. From the initial attempts during the early sixteenth century, nearly 350 years passed before the difficult passage was conquered.

In 1878–1879, a Scandinavian explorer, A. E. Nordenskiöld and his vessel, the *Vega*, sailed from the Atlantic Ocean to the Pacific, following the northern coast of Eurasia. This route has been used by Russians since 1934 for both military and commercial purposes. It is now kept open during the winter months using powerful atomic-powered icebreakers.

Race to the Poles

By the dawn of the twentieth century, a race was under way to be the first to reach the North and South poles. Although these adventures are of historic and scientific interest, they had very little geographic impact other than in the context of exploration itself.

The adventures of such explorers as Robert E. Peary, Roald Amundsen, and Ernest Shackleton are amazing tales of daring, skill, and endurance. Hardships endured by many of them, such as Shackleton and his well-documented struggle to survive, stagger the imagination. Several of the more successful explorers were those adopting Eskimo methods.

American Robert Peary was long believed to have been the first person to reach the North Pole. He reached what he believed to be 90 degrees north latitude in 1909. Much of his success can be attributed to the fact that he had Eskimo guides, used dog sleds, wore Eskimo clothing, lived off the land, and even built igloos. Recent analyses of Peary's records, however, suggest that he fell some 25 miles (40 kilometers) short of his goal. In 1926, American Admiral Richard E. Byrd believed that he flew over the North Pole. His claim, too, is questioned by some skeptics on the basis of evidence drawn from his diaries. The North Pole was not reached on foot until 1968, when Wally Herbert, of Great Britain, finally achieved the feat. The South Pole, though colder, could be reached by land rather than over a rugged and treacherous ice surface. A Norwegian party headed by Roald Amundsen reached 90 degrees south latitude in December 1911 (five years after he had been the first to traverse the Northwest Passage).

EUROPEAN EXPLOITATION AND SETTLEMENT

With but few exceptions, European exploitation and settlement within the Arctic has been recent and temporary. People have been drawn to the region for a variety of reasons. Most "invaders" have been lured to the region hoping to profit from its vast wealth of natural resources. Some came (usually reluctantly) as government administrators or military personnel, or for some other political or strategic reason. Still others came as scientists hoping to unlock the region's many unsolved mysteries. Only during the past century have significant numbers of people come north to make a home and stake their future. The following is a brief discussion of the primary activities that drew Europeans to the Arctic.

Whaling

Whaling brought hunters to northern waters as early as the seventeenth century, and the practice continued as perhaps the chief economic activity until the dawn of the twentieth century. Because it was conducted in open water, whaling had little impact on Polar World landscapes or peoples. Economically, however, it was of great importance. Whale oil (from the blubber, or fat) was a chief source of fuel until replaced by petroleum during the late 1800s. Whalebone (baleen) was used in making corset stays. In some countries, whale was a chief source of meat. Hunting was so successful that many species of whales faced extinction. Today, they are protected by law.

Trapping

The trapping of fur-bearing animals has been important throughout nearly all of the polar region for centuries. It was furs, you will recall, that drew the Cossacks across Siberia to the shores of the Bering Strait by 1650. From the seas came the valuable pelts of seals, walruses, and sea otters. A variety of land animals, including Arctic fox, sable, and beaver (only in the taiga forests), also contributed greatly to what became an economic mainstay of the region. The fur trade brought Europeans and native peoples together, often for the first time. Trade routes were opened, forts and trading posts sprouted in the wilderness, and commercial enterprises such as Hudson's Bay Company were established.

The Hudson's Bay Company (HBC) was founded in 1670 at Churchill, on the western shore of Hudson Bay, for two purposes: to trade with Canadian Eskimos and Indians for pelts and to search for the Northwest Passage. The company's owners found the fur trade so lucrative, however, that the quest for the passage was quickly forgotten. HBC played a major role in exploring, charting, and opening northern Canada to settlement and eventually other types of development. Economically, HBC was one of Canada's most powerful economic forces for several centuries. Today, some trapping continues, particularly of seals, but the industry has fallen onto hard times because of changing styles and public sentiment against killing animals.

Fishing

The Grand Banks in the Atlantic Ocean, off the coast of Newfoundland, have long been one of the world's most productive fishing waters. Some historical geographers believe that Portuguese and perhaps other Europeans were fishing these waters long before Columbus's epic voyage. Today, commercial fishing has fallen on hard times. Overharvesting has severely depleted populations of cod, salmon, halibut, and other important species. Nonetheless, waters of the North Atlantic, North Pacific, and Arctic Ocean continue to be among the world's most productive fishing grounds.

Missionaries

As European influences spread across the dark taiga and into the bleak tundra, Christian missionaries followed. Russian Orthodoxy spread across Siberia and into Alaska, where distinctive Orthodox churches and crosses still can be found in some communities. Roman Catholicism and several Protestant faiths are practiced by native peoples throughout much of Northern America.

Minerals

Prospecting for and the extraction of mineral resources is a rather recent development in the Polar World. Both tasks are made difficult by the region's isolation, lack of transportation facilities, distance from markets, and permafrost. These and other factors add to the difficulty and cost of searching for, producing, and transporting minerals. Nonetheless, it is almost certain that the Arctic region holds much of the world's remaining mineral reserves. Its geologic secrets have only recently begun to be revealed, many of them resulting from aerial surveys.

Nothing attracts wealth-seekers like the prospect of finding gold. Rich gold deposits drew prospectors to Alaska and Canada a century ago. "Black gold" (petroleum) continues to be an economic mainstay of this region today. Some of the world's leading deposits of iron, uranium, lead and zinc, petroleum, and natural gas are known to exist in the region.

Strategic Importance

The cold war between the Soviet Union and the United States and its allies catapulted the Polar World into the limelight as a major strategic location. By 1940, developments in navigation made transpolar flight possible and soon thereafter long-range missiles joined the military arsenal. "Great circle" routes crossing the polar region significantly reduced travel distance between North America and Eurasia. (Any great circle route—the shortest distance between two points—can be determined by using a piece of string and a globe. For example, place one end of string on the U.S. Middle West and the other on the Soviet [now Russian] heartland, and it crosses the polar region.) Both the United States and Soviet Union placed a series of radar warning networks and military bases in the Arctic. In North America, many radar stations were staffed by

In 1896, gold was discovered in the Klondike region of Canada, and over the next couple of years approximately 100,000 people made the treacherous journey north in search of riches. Pictured here is a camp at Lake Bennett, in British Columbia, during the construction of the White Pass and Yukon Railroad in 1897, which connected Skagway, Alaska, and Whitehorse, Yukon.

Inuit or other Native Americans. American military bases also extended from the Aleutians to Greenland.

Polar Scientific Research

Because of its unique conditions, the polar regions have long intrigued scientists. Much of the research has focused on various aspects of the natural environment, but human activities such as agriculture, developing and testing cold weather gear, and transportation have all been studied extensively. Because so much of their country lies in the Arctic or sub-Arctic zone, Russians have long been world leaders in cold-lands research. Billions of research dollars have been spent in the study of permafrost alone.

Several countries have research stations in Antarctica. Scientists are fascinated by the continent and its many secrets. Antarctic geology, properties of ice, and the tolerance of various materials and types of equipment to extreme cold are some of the things studied. Cores drilled through the continent's icecaps reveal much about past climates and composition of the atmosphere. Antarctica may even help reveal mysteries of the universe—scientists have found the continent's ice to be a treasure chest of meteorites!

Political Administrators

As midlatitude economic involvement in the Arctic grew, the region also began to be drawn into the sphere of outside political control. Military personnel, police, and others were assigned to remote northern outposts to safeguard American, Canadian, and Russian interests. Today, all Arctic lands are either independent (as is Iceland), semi-independent territories (such as Denmark's Greenland), or simply a part of some country (as Alaska, the Canadian north, or Siberia are).

CHANGES IN ABORIGINAL WAY OF LIFE

The old Polar World way of life is gone forever, and in many ways, this is sad. Change, however, has removed much of the harshness from Arctic living. All native peoples of the region have experienced at least a partial loss of their aboriginal culture. Few, if any of them, however, would want to return to their traditional way of living, or the life experienced before Europeans arrived. Change has occurred at different times in different places. Europeans arrived centuries ago in Iceland, southern Greenland, coastal Labrador, around Hudson Bay, and in parts of northern Eurasia. Some remote groups, on the other hand, were not reached by midlatitude peoples or their cultural influences until well into the twentieth century.

Culture change is always accompanied by turmoil, unrest, and social upheaval (a reality well illustrated by the experience of Native American peoples in the United States). Religion, for example, is the single most important element of many cultures. It can govern nearly every aspect of people's lives. When Europeans introduced new Christian faiths, the very foundation of many traditional societies was stripped away. Europeans also introduced many diseases, against which New World peoples had no resistance. In some extreme cases, entire populations were wiped out.

Europeans also introduced jobs and a cash economy. Within a single generation, many native peoples were forced to make a huge economic change. Traditionally, they were self-sufficient. They lived off the land, practicing a folk economy in which hunting, fishing, and gathering provided their needs. Europeans, however, brought wage-paying jobs to the region. Suddenly, natives were thrown into a commercial economy based on employment and cash. With money to spend, they no longer needed to do those things for themselves that their fore-fathers had done for millenia. Rarely in all of human history have a people undergone such extreme culture change—and cultural shock—in such a short period of time.

The introduction of the rifle serves as an excellent example of the impact a single new technology can have on a culture. The rifle, perhaps more than any other material trait of a culture, helped destroy traditional Inuit culture (as well as that of many other Polar World peoples). For thousands of years, Eskimo males devoted much of their time to hunting. About a century ago, rifles became available (for cash payment). Armed, a hunter could kill, in a very short time, enough seals, caribou, or other game to provide food and clothing to his family for an entire year. In many places, game animals even became scarce and in some locations extinct.

What would hunters now do with all their newly found spare time? With cash, of course, came stores, where not only guns and ammunition could be purchased, but many other items as well—including alcohol. With so much idle time, natives turned to drink, and drinking (and later drugs) became an epidemic. In some villages, up to 90 percent of all males are alcohol or drug dependent. Throughout much of the region, these conditions are the leading cause of death (followed closely by suicide). Suicide rates in Arctic native villages rank the highest in the world. In addition, store-bought food has caused many health problems never before experienced by Arctic peoples. Diabetes, cancer, and heart-related diseases have increased tremendously. So have obesity, tooth decay, and digestive problems. Store-bought shoes and clothing are no match for frigid Arctic temperatures. Today, for the first time ever, many natives suffer from frostbite!

Change is inevitable in a rapidly evolving world in which "progress" has assumed the importance of a sacred mantra. Time, it is said, cannot stand still; neither can cultures. For many traditional societies, however, change comes with a tremendous price tag—the loss of cultural identity. Today, many Polar World people own basically the same electronic gadgets and conveniences that people from midlatitudes possess. On the other hand, imagine yourself living in a village of several hundred people, with no link to your closest neighbors, who are located several hundred miles away. In the modern world, extreme isolation (whether social, cultural, or physical), with its accompanying loneliness, is one of the chief problems faced by many remote cultures. We will discuss some of these issues in the next chapter.

7

Contemporary Conditions and Regions

M ost of the polar realm remains geographically remote. It is also a huge blank spot on the global "mental map" of most North Americans. Nonetheless, it is a region of growing importance and increasing attention. Most Americans are aware of the heated Arctic National Wildlife Refuge (ANWR) controversy—which is most important, petroleum or wildlife habitat? Canadians certainly are aware of native (both Inuit and First Nations) drives toward political independence. Will the success realized by the Inuit in gaining their own semiautonomous territory be played out by others elsewhere? What percentage of Earth's remaining mineral wealth lays locked away in the frozen tundra? These are just some of the questions that are beginning to be asked with increasing frequency.

CONTEMPORARY CONDITIONS

Problems relating to social and cultural change have been discussed previously. Here, attention is focused on such conditions as the region's sparse population, isolation, economic development, and political trends.

A Sparse Population

Polar World lands occupy about 16 percent of Earth's surface, yet the region is home to only an estimated 8 million people. Excluding Antarctica, the land area drops to 7 percent of Earth's surface, whereas the population figure remains the same. This amounts to about .0012 percent of all humans living in an area nearly twice the size of the lower 48 U.S. states! Expressed in density, the Arctic region has about two people per square mile (less than one per kilometer). Density figures, of course, are extremely misleading. Vast areas remain totally uninhabited, whereas several Russian Arctic cities have populations exceeding 200,000.

Extreme Isolation

Isolation remains a tremendous problem throughout most of the Arctic. Permafrost, surface lakes and streams, spongy muskeg (marshes), and other obstacles severely limit land travel. Ice ridges, open leads, and other hazards limit travel over ice. Few rivers are navigable. Except in Scandinavia and western European Russia, not a single railroad penetrates the region, and only one road—the Dalton Highway from Fairbanks to Alaska's Prudhoe Bay—crosses the tundra to reach the Arctic shore. Siberia, an area roughly the size of the lower 48 U.S. states, has not a single mile of road for automobiles! Nearly all travel within the Arctic is either by modern aircraft or the ancient technology of dog or reindeer sled! (During recent decades, traditional means of travel have rapidly given way to snowmobiles.)

On the other hand, today, most of the region has access to satellite-based telecommunications. Television, radio, telephone, and in some places even Internet communications now deliver news, information, and entertainment to even the most remote communities.

These conveniences, though serving as a link to the outside, are a mixed blessing. Realizing what life is like on the "outside" can create expectations and desires that cannot be fulfilled in the remote villages. This is a particularly critical problem for many young people. Some studies suggest that the resulting frustrations are partially responsible for the tragically high suicide rates among young adults. In addition, many youngsters are raised in the sheltered environment of a closely knit traditional society and remote village. Should they move to a city, they often lack the knowledge, experience, and social skills needed to successfully adapt to urban jobs and lifestyles.

Conditions Contributing to Development

As discussed in the preceding chapter, people have come to the Arctic for a variety of reasons. In the polar realm and elsewhere, people are drawn to opportunity, particularly the prospect of economic gain. In turn, development (transportation, commerce, various services, and other amenities) follows people and money. Obviously, all three elements—economic potential, population growth, and regional development—are closely intertwined.

In Alaska, for example, the Prudhoe Bay petroleum project nearly doubled the state's population. As a result, the state's economy boomed, as did development of various kinds (for instance, building the very costly highway to Prudhoe Bay became economically justified). Most Alaskan communities of any size now offer the same amenities and services that one would expect to find in the "lower 48" states.

Economic Potentials and Problems

Just as society and culture are changing throughout the Polar World, so, too, are the region's economic and political structures. Resource-hungry midlatitude peoples are gazing increasingly toward the Arctic as a possible source of metals, fuels, and timber. Huge reserves of many resources are known to exist. In some instances, they are already being extracted.

The Trans-Alaska pipeline winds its way through the interior of Alaska, from Prudhoe Bay in the north to Valdez in the south. The pipeline travels 800 miles (1,290 kilometers) and has transported more than 15 billion barrels of oil since it was completed in 1977.

Examples include rich deposits of iron ore in Labrador and northern Sweden, petroleum in Alaska, and natural gas in western Siberia.

Throughout much of the region, however, production is not yet economically feasible. Developing resources such as mines, oil fields, or timber is both difficult and extremely expensive in the Arctic. Even where production may be feasible, throughout most of the region the cost of transporting resources to market would be extremely difficult and costly. The Trans-Alaska Pipeline, which is 800 miles (1,290 kilometers) in length, cost $8 billion to construct, or $1 million per mile ($390,000 per kilometer)!

Economic development faces many other challenges, as well. Low populations mean a lack of laborers. Nearly the entire workforce involved in developing Alaska's petroleum resources was brought in from the lower 48 states. This, of course, is extremely costly. In 2006, the average annual salary of an employee in Alaska's oil and gas industry was about $100,000. Canada and Russia face similar challenges in developing petroleum and natural gas reserves.

Political Integration

Political geographers have long realized that it is difficult for governments to control remote regions, and they do so with limited access. In order to gain favor of voters, governments must devote most resources to areas where the greatest number of people will benefit. Why spend money on "them" living "way out there"? This problem is magnified when those living far away from effective national control are of a different culture. Most of the Polar World meets both conditions. It is little wonder, then, that many native groups have sought or are seeking greater independence. In fact, it is a problem that in varying degrees plagues all seven countries that have territory and citizens living in the Polar World.

THE AMERICAN REALM

The American realm of the Polar World includes Alaska, Canada, and Greenland. Inuit is the dominant native culture from Alaska to eastern Greenland. Smaller groups of Aleut and Indians (by various preferred names) also inhabit the region. Population is extremely sparse, with no more than 250,000 people inhabiting an area of about 2 million square miles (5.2 million square kilometers). To visualize this distribution, imagine the population of Bakersfield, California, or Lexington, Kentucky, spread out across the United States, west of the Mississippi River!

Alaska

Paradoxically, Alaska almost certainly was the first place in the Americas to be reached by Old World peoples—yet the state proudly boasts of being the "Last Frontier." Alaska was admitted to the union as the forty-ninth state in 1959. Roughly the northern half of the state lies within the Polar World. Fairbanks, a modern city with a population of about 35,000, is the continent's northernmost large urban center. It lies at the southern edge of the Polar World.

Natural resources have always been the backbone of the Alaskan economy. Between 1850 and 1915, thousands of prospectors headed north to Nome, the Kenai Peninsula, the Fairbanks area, and elsewhere to seek their fortune in gold. During recent decades, as was discussed earlier, petroleum has spurred the state's economy and population growth. In 1977, oil began to flow from Prudhoe Bay to Valdez, a port on the Gulf of Alaska, through the Trans-Alaska Pipeline.

The state's petroleum-based economic future depends upon decisions made thousands of miles away, in Washington, D.C. An estimated 5 to 11 billion barrels of oil are believed to lie beneath the tundra of the Arctic National Wildlife Refuge. People concerned about safeguarding ANWR's pristine environment are opposed to opening the refuge to drilling (even though it would affect only about 2 to 3 percent of the total area). They are concerned about such problems as pollution and disturbing the calving grounds of the Porcupine caribou herd. Others are more worried about the nation's dependence upon foreign oil sources and the price of gasoline. They, of course, want to drill. In December 2005, the Senate once again voted against development—at least for the time being.

The controversy is stirring a heated local debate, as well. Coastal Inupiat Eskimos strongly support drilling. For three decades, they have benefited immensely from Alaska's North Slope oil boom. Now, with Prudhoe Bay production in decline, these locals are eager to see the ANWR reserves tapped. They believe drilling in ANWR will help the region's economy to continue to prosper. Inland, however, the 7,000 or so Gwich'in Indians are strongly opposed to development. For thousands of years, they have depended on caribou meat, which they eat almost daily, as the mainstay of their diet. Much of their culture, in fact, is tied in one way or another to the region's now-dwindling and increasingly threatened caribou herds. If the caribou die out, so will much of their traditional culture.

Canada

The Canadian Arctic occupies an area of roughly one million square miles (2.5 million square kilometers), a region about the size of the United States, east of the Mississippi River. Much of the land is low-lying and relatively flat. In many places, more than 60 percent of the surface is covered with water during the summer months. Surface travel under such conditions is all but impossible. Only one road penetrates the region. The Dempster Highway reaches Inuvik, a town of about 3,200 people located 140 miles north of the Arctic Circle, near the mouth of the Mackenzie River. Most of the region is accessible only by air or, in some locations, by water (or on winter ice).

Natural resources have been the key to both native and European economic survival in the region. Native peoples depended upon marine life and game animals such as the caribou for their survival. Early Europeans were attracted to the rich fishing banks off Canada's east coast, possibly even before Columbus's voyage. By the seventeenth century, fur-bearing animals became the focus of economic attention. By 1670, the Hudson's Bay Company (HBC) was organized at Churchill, on the western shore of Hudson Bay. Its network spread throughout much of Canada, and HBC soon became one of the country's most powerful and influential corporations.

Yukon, Klondike, and Dawson are well-known names in Canada and beyond. In 1896, gold was discovered along the Yukon and Klondike rivers. The Klondike gold rush drew prospectors from throughout the world. Because of the rush, the community of Dawson prospered. At its peak, the city's population soared to 40,000, making it Canada's largest community west of Winnipeg, Manitoba! Mining, however, is a boom-and-bust economic activity, particularly in a cold, remote region. When the ores began to run out, the population

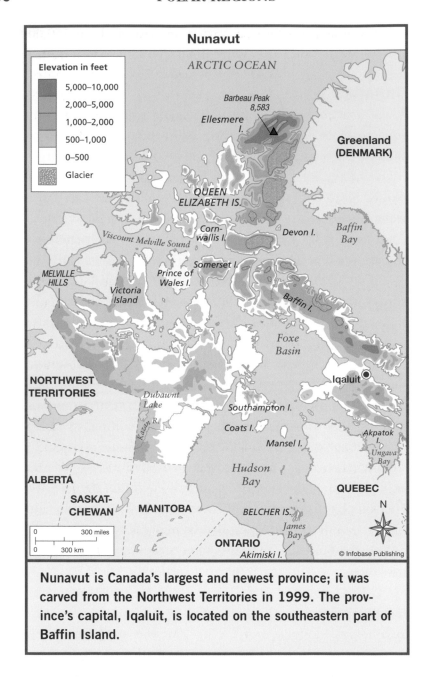

Nunavut

Elevation in feet

	5,000–10,000
	2,000–5,000
	1,000–2,000
	500–1,000
	0–500
	Glacier

ARCTIC OCEAN

Barbeau Peak
8,583

Ellesmere I.

Greenland
(DENMARK)

QUEEN
ELIZABETH IS.

Corn-
wallis I.

Viscount Melville Sound

Devon I.

Baffin
Bay

MELVILLE
HILLS

Somerset I.

Prince of
Wales I.

Victoria
Island

Baffin I.

Foxe
Basin

NORTHWEST
TERRITORIES

Dubawnt
Lake

Kazan R.

Southampton I.

Iqaluit

Coats I.

Akpatok
I.

Mansel I.

Ungava
Bay

ALBERTA

Hudson
Bay

QUEBEC

SASKAT-
CHEWAN

MANITOBA

BELCHER IS.

N

James
Bay

0	300 miles
0	300 km

ONTARIO

Akimiski I.

© Infobase Publishing

Nunavut is Canada's largest and newest province; it was carved from the Northwest Territories in 1999. The province's capital, Iqaluit, is located on the southeastern part of Baffin Island.

sharply declined. Today, Dawson is a community of about 2,000 people, who rely primarily on a thriving summer tourist trade and memories of a bygone golden era.

Imagine a territory occupying an area of about 750,000 square miles (2 million square kilometers)—the size of western Europe, or nearly three times the size of Texas—with a population of only 29,000. Stretch the territory over nearly 2,000 miles (3,000 kilometers), in both north-south and east-west directions. If this territory were a country, it would have the world's lowest population density, even lower than Greenland. Now, take about half the area and scatter it over several dozen large islands and hundreds of smaller ones. No railroads or highways reach the territory, and water access is frozen over during much of the year. Most of the area can be reached only by plane, or by ship during the short summer. The capital and largest city is home to about 6,000 people. Politically, however, the capital is at a great disadvantage because it is located on a remote island perched at the very edge of the territory. It has very little economic activity and depends heavily on support from the country of which it is a part. Welcome to Nunavut and its capital city, Iqaluit!

Nunavut is a political and ethnic experiment on a grand scale. It was carved out of the Northwest Territories in 1999 as an Inuit-governed territory. About 85 percent of the population is native, and most are Inuit. In fact, the name *Nunavut* means "our land" in the Inuit language. Despite its many unique and seemingly insurmountable hurdles, the citizens of Nunavut and Iqualuit are eager to show that they can govern their own land—and they are very optimistic that they will succeed!

Greenland

Northwestern Greenland lies only 16 miles (26 kilometers) from the northern tip of Nunavut's Ellsemere Island. More than 80 percent of the island lies buried beneath the world's second-largest glacial ice cap. Its 56,000 people, about 85 percent of whom are Inuit, live in widely scattered small villages clinging to the coast. A quarter of all Greenlanders live in the capital, Nuuk (formerly Godthab), located on the southwestern coast. In 1979, Greenland freed itself from Danish control to become a self-governing territory. Denmark continues to control Greenland's foreign affairs.

The View From Iqaluit, Nunavut's Capital City

Nunavut's capital and largest city, Iqaluit, is home to about 6,000 people. Perhaps no capital in the world is at a greater disadvantage in terms of its location—it is located on remote and frigid Baffin Island and at the very far eastern edge of the territory it governs. Other than its governing function, the city has very little economic activity. It must depend heavily upon support from the Canadian government. Nonetheless, as the following comments from the city's official Web site suggest, the residents of Iqaluit are very optimistic that they will succeed.

It's hard to imagine anywhere in Canada with greater prospects. The city's alive with the anything's-possible attitude of a young community. Bursting with new growth [and] exciting economic and social opportunities, this bustling Arctic capital is home to a diverse mix of people enjoying the leading edge of development and phenomenal potential. Young and old are working to create a future that will preserve the strengths of traditional culture, while embracing the surging changes of the 21st century.

Even though it's located on the remote Arctic tundra, Iqaluit aims to be every inch a capital city, with the amenities and quality of life to rival any in Canada. Iqaluit's economy—based mainly on a government that has expanded rapidly since the city became the capital of Nunavut in 1999—is growing by leaps and bounds. The city's infrastructure is developing at a steady clip, trying to catch up with population growth. As well as being Canada's newest and

Several settlements in northwestern Greenland are the world's northernmost permanently occupied communities. The United States, in cooperation with several other countries, main-

most northerly capital, Iqaluit is also Canada's fastest-growing community.*

* Available online at the Official Government Web site of the City of Iqaluit: *www.city.iqaluit.nu.ca/*

Iqaluit is home to about 6,000 people (60 percent of whom are Inuit). The town has an Arctic climate—temperatures stay below freezing for eight months a year and it receives less than 20 inches (500 millimeters) of precipitation annually.

tains its northernmost (near 77 degrees north latitude) military facility, Thule Air Base, on Greenland's northwest coast.

Most of Greenland's economy is based on government aid. For centuries, most Greenlanders turned to the sea, where they depended on fish, whales, seals, and other marine life for their survival. This tradition continues today; fish and shrimp make up about 95 percent of the country's exports. Many people would enjoy visiting Greenland. In addition to its Inuit culture, the island offers a unique environment and some of the world's most spectacular scenery. Unfortunately, the tourist industry is very limited. The season is short, there are few tourist facilities, and travel to and around the island is extremely expensive.

THE EURASIAN REALM

Northern portions of Norway, Sweden, Finland, and Russia lie partially within the Eurasian realm of the Polar World. The area covered is similar to that of the American realm, as are general environmental conditions in the respective regions. Several major differences between the two realms do stand out, however. First, more than 90 percent of all Polar World people reside in Eurasia and about 75 percent of them in Russia. Second, cultural diversity is considerably greater in Eurasia than in the Americas. Finally, portions of the Eurasian Arctic are much better developed than are most areas of the American realm.

Samiland (Lappland)

Samiland occupies northern parts of Norway, Sweden, Finland, and Russia's Kola Peninsula. The region is home to the Sami, formerly called Lapps or Lapplanders, who, for several thou-sand years, have carried the nickname "The reindeer people." At one time, nearly all Samis were nomadic and depended on the reindeer for their survival. You will recall that reindeer, unlike their caribou cousins, are domesticated animals. They are milked, ridden, herded like cattle or sheep, and they pull sleds.

Although only approximately 10 percent of the Sami people still practice reindeer herding, some still take tourists on sleigh rides or photograph them alongside the animals. Pictured here are two tourists in the Finland town of Muonio with two Samis.

Traditionally, during winter months, the Samis lived in stationary settlements located inland, usually within the shelter of the dense taiga forest. There, they were protected from the fierce winds, and plenty of wood was available for building and for fuel. As conditions began to warm and daylight lengthen, a sense of restlessness set in. Families gathered their herds, secured their belongings on a reindeer-pulled sled, and began a centuries-old custom: the annual nomadic trek, in search of better pastures for their reindeer. Nomads have never "just wandered." Rather, they are keenly aware of where good grazing conditions can be found for their herds. In Samiland, the migration was to the coast, where lush grasslands can be found during the summer months. Then, with the approaching darkness and cold of winter, they once again turned inland to the taiga.

Today, an estimated 85,000 Samis inhabit the region, about half of whom live in Norway. Of all Polar World regions, Samiland is the most densely settled, the most accessible, and the best developed economically. As might be expected under such conditions, European Scandinavians and native peoples have long been in contact with one another. This has resulted in a sharp decline in the traditional Sami culture during the past century. Today, for example, very few Samis are involved in any way with reindeer—other, perhaps, than taking tourists on a sleigh ride, or allowing themselves to be photographed next to one of the animals. Because this cultural loss is now recognized, many efforts are now under way to restore and promote Sami language and culture.

Mining, particularly of rich deposits of iron ore at Kiruna, in northern Sweden, and a variety of ores, including copper scattered elsewhere, have boosted the region's economy. Today, tourism—much of which is based on a growing interest in Sami culture and history—is becoming increasingly important.

Russia

It seems unfair to include an area that spans 11 time zones within a single geographic region. Some differences, of course, do exist within the Russian Arctic. For example, European Russia is more accessible and better developed than is most of Siberia. The way reindeer are used (herded in the west, hunted in the east) varies, as well.

Much of the region, however, remains a huge "blank spot" on most peoples' (including geographers') "mental map." During the Soviet era, little if any information was available on this or any other part of the USSR. Siberia also remains the world's largest area (outside of Antarctica) of very low population density. Finally, not a single road or railroad exists in the entire Siberian Arctic. Much of the area has never been seen by people of European culture, except from planes or in satellite images.

As was discussed in Chapter 5, the Siberian Arctic is home to a number of different native peoples. Because of their isolation and information blackout during the Soviet era, little is known about them. Geographers Bella Bychkova-Jordan (who is native to the Sakha Republic) and her husband, the late Terry Jordan-Bychkov, wrote a splendid book describing the region and a Siberian village in great detail.

With few exceptions, cities hug the coast. Murmansk, with an estimated population of 310,000, is the Polar World's largest city. Because of the warm North Atlantic Drift, the sea remains relatively ice-free throughout the year. As a result, the city is an important port for the Russian Navy and is also used commercially. To the east, in the coal-producing Pechora Basin, located near the northern tip of the Ural Mountains, is Vorkuta. The city had a rather notorious origin, having been built in the early 1930s as a *GULAG* (an acronym for the Russian term for Soviet concentration camp). Economically, Vorkuta was an important mining community. Because of high costs, though, the mines closed during the 1990s, and the city's population has dwindled from a high of perhaps 225,000 to the most recent (1989) figure, 116,000. Obviously, a community located north of the Arctic Circle will have difficulty attracting residents. Add to this problem a history of prison camp brutality and closed coal mines, and the city's large drop in population is easily understood!

Moving across the Urals into Siberia, the first Arctic city of any size is Salekhard. Founded in 1595, the community of about 32,000 is a seaport located near the mouth of the Ob River. In addition to serving as a river port, Salekhard has lumber mills, fish canneries, and shipyards. To the east, near (but not on) the mouth of the Yenisey River, is the city of Norilsk. The urban center of about 175,000 people holds two distinctions: It is Russia's northernmost large city and, after Murmansk, the world's second-largest city north of the Arctic Circle. Mining, natural gas, and hydroelectric production are the primary economic activities of the area. From the Yenisey River eastward across the vast expanses of frigid Siberia, there are very few communities. Those that do exist are regional administrative centers, Russian military bases, or towns of some local or regional economic importance.

All of Siberia, and certainly the portion lying in the Polar World, offers tremendous resources and other potentials for development. The area has been home to humans for tens of thousands of years. Obviously, people can and do live here. Russia has a long way to go, however, before Siberia can be made an attractive place to live.

As this chapter draws to a close, let us journey a bit farther eastward to the Bering Strait. Here, we will have come full cycle in our hurried west-to-east trip through the Polar World's various regions. For decades, the West and East (dominated by the United States and the Soviet Union) were locked in the struggle of the cold war. Economically, politically, and socially, the antagonists were worlds apart. In the Bering Strait, though, there are two very small islands: Big Diomede and Little Diomede. The larger island belonged to the USSR (now Russia) and the smaller, as a part of Alaska, to the United States. What is most amazing about the islands is that they lie only about 2.5 miles (4 kilometers) apart. Also, during even the most heated years of the cold war, native peoples passed freely between the islands—and the two countries.

8

Future Prospects for the Polar World

"The future is hard to predict," according to baseball legend Yogi Berra, "because it hasn't happened yet!" This certainly is true with regard to predicting what is likely to happen in the Polar World during coming decades. There simply are too many unanswered questions: Will the earth continue to warm? Will the Atlantic "conveyor belt" break down and plunge the Arctic region into another ice age? What impact might continued population growth have on migration to the Arctic? Will it become economically feasible to reach and extract more of the region's many natural resources? Will new resource deposits be discovered? How will the growing desire by native peoples to be self-governing affect the region's political landscape? What does the future hold in terms of native cultures? Will they be able to adapt contemporary lifestyles while retaining many valued aspects of their own ancient cultures? These are just a few of the questions that must be asked with regard to the polar region's future.

THREAT OF TEMPERATURES WARMING

Climatic change is part of nature's many ongoing cycles. Ice ages come and go, each followed by a period of extreme warming. In times past, Earth has been much warmer than it is today. During the 1970s, when global temperature records were first being compiled, many scientists were predicting the onset of another ice age! Now Earth is warming at a rapid rate, and temperatures are rising in the Polar World twice as fast as they are elsewhere. Whether it is occurring as result of a normal climatic cycle (or cycles) or because of human pollution of the atmosphere is not yet confirmed. In addition, some scientists now see signs of a possible link between global warming and global cooling. As atmospheric heating causes glacial ice to melt, freshwater is added to the North Atlantic. This, they fear, may cause the Gulf Stream and North Atlantic Drift to weaken or even disappear. Were this to happen, much of the Northern Hemisphere and particularly northern Europe could experience a catastrophic drop in temperatures.

If, indeed, warming is occurring, higher temperatures will bring many changes to the Arctic. On the positive side, northern waters—including the Northwest and Northeast Passages—will be open to navigation much of the year. Negative effects seem to heavily outweigh the positive, however. The dire consequences of thawing permafrost have been discussed elsewhere. Sea ice will thin in some places and disappear in others. Polar bears may disappear entirely, and walruses and seals, upon which many native peoples have long depended, may decline in number. Melting glaciers will cause a worldwide rise in sea level. If all ice were to melt, the oceans would rise about 200 feet (60 meters). Many fertile coastal plains would be under water, as would a number of the world's great cities. Thawed surfaces, reduced permafrost, and melted sea ice would make both summer and winter land travel all but impossible in many places. There would be huge changes in the plant and animal life of the Arctic region.

In recent years, warming temperatures have begun to take a toll on the Arctic region. Melting glaciers, warmer water temperatures, and the thawing of permafrost are all signs that the Arctic environment is beginning to be adversely affected.

RESOURCE EXPLOITATION AND ENVIRONMENTAL DAMAGE

Harvesting the region's abundant store of natural resources almost certainly will continue to be the chief source of economic development and human settlement within the region. Nearly all areas of the Polar World have one or more resources that can be tapped when needed. As the world population grows, so will the need for additional resources (and living space). It is very likely that during the twenty-first century, midlatitude peoples will be looking northward for both. In the past, people have looked at the Arctic as a remote frontier, about which they cared little. The attitude has been one of "If it is damaged, so what?" The development of the Arctic has caused many problems. The environment is fragile and very slow to mend when damaged. Vehicle tracks across a tundra surface, for example, can be visible for decades. As more people are drawn to the region and more pressure is placed on the environment, often irreparable damage increases as well. Waters are polluted, vegetation and animal life are threatened, and forests are destroyed.

CHANGING NATIVE CULTURES

Certainly changes in traditional ways of life that have taken place during the past century will continue at an accelerated pace. People may look to their past with a longing for the "good old days," but few if any would really want to return to them and their many hardships. What will happen—and there are many signs that it is already occurring—is that people will begin taking great pride in their culture's traditions. They will teach their language in schools, as are the Samis and in some places the Inuit. Many folkways, such as arts and music, will be preserved. Museums will take pride in displaying traditional items that were used by the people in times past. Universities will begin teaching courses focusing upon the traditional culture. The people themselves, however, will become increasingly integrated into the contemporary cultural mainstream.

CHANGING POLITICAL LANDSCAPES

It is quite doubtful that any major changes will occur in the primary political landscape of the region, that is, the countries themselves. Canada is the one giant question mark in this regard. What would happen to the rest of Canada, particularly the eastern Maritime Provinces, if French Quebec gained its independence? It is possible that within several countries, some political changes will occur. What the Canadian Inuit achieved in gaining some political autonomy may happen elsewhere.

Politically, the region gained strategic military, hence political, importance during the cold war, when the United States and the Soviet Union menacingly faced one another across the Arctic Ocean. Today, the region's military significance is being replaced by its civilian importance. International airlines regularly fly polar routes. If you ship a parcel by air to a destination in Africa, Asia, Australia, or Europe, chances are it will go to Anchorage, Alaska, for further routing.

ECONOMIC DEVELOPMENT AND POPULATION GROWTH

By 2050, the world's population is projected to reach 9 to 10 billion, nearly half as many people as inhabit our planet today. Where will they turn for space, resources, opportunity, and a future? People have lived in the Arctic region for thousands of years. Cities such as Fairbanks, Alaska—located just a few degrees south of the Arctic Circle—are modern in every way. People can live comfortably in the Arctic. They simply need a reason to do so: development of some kind.

Taking a final peek into the crystal ball in an attempt to foresee the Polar World's future, the northern mists begin to vanish, and another vision begins to appear. As the sea smoke fades, the image clears: The world's "Last Frontier" is on the brink of becoming the twenty-first century's "Land of Opportunity."

Historical Geography
at a Glance

75,000–12,000 YBP*	Glacial ice covers much of Polar World.
35,000 YBP	Humans are present in the Arctic coastal region, near the mouth of the Tana River in northeastern Siberia.
Pre-12,000 YBP	Humans migrate from Asia to the Americas for the first time; dates vary greatly, with some evidence suggesting that humans may have crossed Beringia, possibly closely following the coast, rather than through an "ice-free corridor," as early as perhaps 40,000 years ago.
12,000–10,000 YBP	Glacial ice caps and sheets attain approximately their present-day distribution.
325 B.C.	Greek explorer Pytheas travels north to a land he called Thule believed by some to possibly have been coastal Norway, near the Arctic Circle.
A.D. 984	Vikings reach Greenland.
1000	Vikings reach "Vineland the Good" (North America).
1003	Vikings settle at village called Hop, believed to have been L'Anse aux Meadows, Newfoundland.
1581	Russian Cossacks cross the Ural Mountains and conquer the Kingdom of Sibir.
1500–1600	Following Columbus's voyages, a number of European explorers begin the search for a water passageway, through or around the Americas, to the Far East; much of the resulting exploration

	focuses on the quest for a northwest or north-east passage.
1600s–1900s	Commercial whaling in Arctic waters is popular.
1608–1609	Henry Hudson searches for Northwest Passage and discovers bay bearing his name; his crew mutinies, and he is set adrift and lost.
1650	Russians reach Bering Strait.
1670	Hudson's Bay Company formed in Canada, with headquarters at Churchill, on the shores of Hudson Bay.
1850–1915	Thousands of fortune seekers flood Alaska and Canada's Yukon and Klondike river valleys after gold is discovered.
1867	United States purchases Alaska from Russia for $7.2 million, in a transaction that came to be called "Seward's Folly."
1878–1879	Scandinavian explorer A. E. Nordenskiöld, on his vessel, the *Vega*, makes first trips through the Northeast Passage, sailing from the Atlantic Ocean to the Pacific following the northern coast of Eurasia; this route has been used by Russians since 1934.
1903–1906	Norwegian Roald Amundsen, on his ship, the *Göja*, finally navigates the Northwest Passage.
1909	American Robert E. Peary believes he has reached the North Pole; subsequent research suggests that he fell short of his goal.
1911	A Norwegian party headed by Roald Amundsen is first to reach the South Pole.
1940	Advances in technology make flying polar routes possible, thereby considerably shortening the distance between North America and Eurasia.
1959	Alaska admitted to the union as the forty-ninth state.

1968 Wally Herbert, of Great Britain, becomes first person to actually reach the North Pole on foot.

1977 Oil begins flowing through Trans-Alaska Pipeline from Prudhoe Bay on the Arctic coast to Valdez on the Gulf of Alaska.

1979 Greenland gains semiautonomy from Denmark.

1999 Nunavut becomes an Inuit-governed Canadian territory.

2000 "B-15" ice island with an area of about 4,500 square miles (11,655 square kilometers) breaks away from Antarctica's Ross Ice Shelf.

* years before present

Bibliography

Armstrong, Terence, George Rogers, and Graham Rowley. *The Circumpolar North*. London: Methuen, 1978.

Baird, Patrick D. *The Polar World*. New York: John Wiley, 1965.

Berreby, David. "Running on Tundra." *Discover* (June 1996): pp. 74–81.

Bruemmer, Fred. "Life Upon the Permafrost." *Natural History* (April 1987): pp. 31–39.

Walker, Harley J. *Man in the Arctic: The Changing Nature of His Quest for Food and Water as Related to Snow, Ice, and Permafrost*. ADTIC Publication A-107. Maxwell Air Force Base, Alabama: Arctic, Desert, Tropic Information Center Research Studies Institute, 1962.

Wallace, Scott. "ANWR: the Great Divide." *Smithsonian* (October, 2005): pp. 48–56.

Further Reading

Bychkova-Jordan, Bella, and T. G. Jordan-Bychkov. *Siberian Village: Land and Life in the Sakha Republic*. Minneapolis: University of Minnesota Press, 2001.

Dando, William A., et al. *Russia second edition*. Philadelphia: Chelsea House, 2007.

Desaulniers, Kristi L. *Canada*. Philadelphia: Chelsea House, 2003.

Freuchen, Peter. *Book of the Eskimos*. New York: Bramhall House, 1961.

Henry, J. David. "Northern Exposure." *Natural History* (February 2005): pp. 27–32.

Jenness, Diamond. *The People of the Twilight*. Chicago: University of Chicago Press, 1959 (reprint of 1928 1/e).

Kimble, G.H.T., and Dorothy Good, eds. *Geography of the Northlands*. New York: American Geographical Society and John Wiley, 1955.

MacQuarrie, Bob. *The Northern Circumpolar World*. Edmonton, Alberta: Reidmore Books, 1996.

McNeese, Tim. *The Yukon River*. Philadelphia: Chelsea House, 2004.

Nansen, Fridtjob. *In Northern Mists: Arctic Exploration in Early Times*. London: W. Heinemann, 1911.

Nordenskjold, Otto, and L. Mecking. *The Geography of Polar Regions*. New York: American Geographical Society, 1928.

Pelto, Pertti J. *The Snowmobile Revolution: Technology and Social Change in the Arctic*. Menlo Park, Calif.: Benjamin/Cummings, 1973.

Riches, David. *Northern Nomadic Hunters-Gatherers*. London: Academic Press, 1982.

Sandness, Roger K., and C. F. Gritzner. *Iceland*. Philadelphia: Chelsea House, 2003.

Sauer, Carl O. *Northern Mists*. Berkeley and Los Angeles: University of California Press, 1968.

Smith, Kathleen Lopp, ed. *Ice Window: Letters from a Bering Strait Village, 1892–1902*. Fairbanks: University of Alaska Press, 2001.

Stefansson, Viljalmur. *Arctic Manual*. New York: Macmillan, 1944.

———. *The Friendly Arctic: The Story of Five Years in Polar Regions*. New York: Macmillan, 1921.

———. *My Life with the Eskimo*. New York: Macmillan, 1951.

WEB SITES

The World Factbook
http://www.cia.gov/cia/publications/factbook/index.html.

Water Science for Schools. Glaciers and Icecaps, Storehouses of Freshwater. USGS Web site.
http://ga.water.usgs.gov/edu/earthglacier.html.

Circumpolar Arctic Geobotanical Atlas
http://www.geobotany.uaf.edu/arcticgeobot.

Who are the Sami? Scandinavica.com Web site
http://www.scandinavica.com/sami.htm.

Frequently Asked Questions About the Aurora: What are the northern lights, the aurora borealis? Athena Curriculum: Space.
http://vathena.arc.nasa.gov/curric/space/aurora/aurofaq1.html.

Picture Credits

page:

Index

A

aborigines. *See* native peoples
adaptations of humans, 7–8, 62–63
advection fog, 29–30
agonic line, 10
Alaska, 80–81, 95, 97–99
alcoholism, 92
Aleuts, 69
algae, 52, 53
alpine glaciers, 40, 49–50
American polar regions. *See* Alaska;
    Canada; Greenland
Americas, first humans in, 64–66
Amundsen, Roald, 83, 85
animal life
    global warming and, 110
    human dependence upon, 54–55,
        68–69, 74
    species present, 54–59
Antarctic Circle, 21
Antarctic ice cap, 37
Antarctica, 8–9, 27, 29
Arctic Circle, 9, 21
Arctic National Wildlife Refuge
    (ANWR), 14–15, 93, 98
Arctic Ocean Basin, 46–47
Arctic Ocean, sea ice in, 40–41
Athabaskan Indians, 69
aurora australis, 32
aurora borealis, 32–33

B

Bering Strait, 64–65, 108
Beringia, 64–65
Berra, Yogi, 109

bird life, 58–59
blizzards, 29, 35
boreal forest. *See* taiga
Bychkova-Jordan, Bella and Terry,
    107
Byrd, Richard E., 85

C

Canada, 99–101, 113
Canadian Archipelago, 47
caribou, 55, 98–99
carnivores, 56–57
climate. *See also* weather
    climactic regions, 17–19
    defined, 16
    precipitation levels, 26–28
    summer and winter conditions,
        23–26
    temperature control factors, 20–22
coastal migration route, 65–66
Columbia Icefield, 38
compass headings, 10–11
construction on permafrost, 43–45
contemporary conditions in polar
    world, 93–97. *See also specific
    regions, e.g.,* Alaska
continental glaciers, 36–40
Corte Real, Gaspar, 82–83
Cossack exploration, 80–81
cultural ecology, 12
culture of native peoples
    characteristics, 68–69
    European influence on, 90–92,
        94–95, 106, 112
    preservation of traditions, 112

D

Dalton Highway, 45, 94
Davis, John, 83
Dawson, Canada, 99–100
Dempster Highway, 99
Denali (Mount McKinley), 47
deserts, 26–27
development, 95–97, 113
diet, Eskimo, 71, 72–73
driftwood, 30–32
drug abuse, 92
drumlins, 49

E

economic development, 95–97, 113
economic structure of native cultures, 69
ecosystems, 52–54
elevation, and temperature, 22
environmental damage, 15, 112
Eric the Red, 79
eskers, 49
Eskimo (Inuit), 7, 34, 67–68, 70–74, 91–92
Eurasia, northwest passage of, 84–85
Eurasian peoples, 74–75
Eurasian polar regions. *See* Russia; Samiland; Siberia
European influences
   on aboriginal way of life, 90–92, 94–95, 106, 112
   early contacts, 77–81
   exploitation and settlement, 76–77, 86–90
   search for Northwest Passage, 81–86
exploration, 13, 76–77, 81–86

F

Fairbanks, Alaska, 98, 113
Far East, search for route to, 81–86
fast (shelf) ice, 41
fauna, 54–59
fishing industry, 87
floe ice, 41
flora, 52–54

fog, 29–30
freshwater reserves of polar region, 40, 42
frigid zone, 9
Frobisher, Martin, 83
fur trade, 86–87
future prospects in polar world, 109–113

G

glacial erratics, 49
glacial ice caps and ice sheets, 17, 36–40
glacial ice, formation of, 20, 36
glacial till, 49, 50
glaciers, 38–40, 48–51
global cooling, 110
global warming, 42, 45, 110–111
Göja, 83
gold prospecting, 88, 98, 99–100
great circle route, 88
Greenland, 47, 79–80, 101–104
ground fog, 29

H

Half Moon, 83
hanging valleys, 50
harpoons, 71
health problems of native peoples, 92
Herbert, Wally, 85
herbivores, 55–56
Hudson, Henry, 83
Hudson Bay, 49
Hudson's Bay Company, 87, 99
hunting, 71, 73
hydrosphere, defined, 33

I

ice. *See also* glaciers
   area coverage by, 36
   glacial ice caps and ice sheets, 36–40
   lake and river ice, 42
   sea ice, 40–42
   travel over, 41–42
   words for, 34

ice age humans, 63–64
ice caps, glacial, 36–40
ice fog, 29
ice islands, 41
ice sheets, glacial, 36–40
icebergs, 38–40
Iditarod Trail Sled Dog Race, 72–73
Indians, 67, 68, 69
insects, 59
Inuit (Eskimo), 7, 34, 67–68, 70–74,
    91–92
Iqaluit, Nunavut, Canada, 101,
    102–103
isolation, 94–95

K

Kalaallit, 68
Klondike gold rush, 99–100

L

lake ice, 42
lakes, 59–60
landforms
    continental, 46–47
    glaciation effects on, 48–51
    landform regions, 47–48
    patterned ground, 51
L'Anse aux Meadows, 80
Lappland (Samiland), 104–106
Lapps (Sami), 67, 68, 74, 106
latitude, and temperature, 20–21
lemmings, 56
lichens, 52, 53
life, distribution of, 51–52. *See also*
    animal life; plant life

M

Mackenzie River, 60
magnetic declination, 11
magnetic north, 10
McKinley, Mount (Denali), 47
migrations of humans to Americas,
    64–66
military significance of Arctic, 88–89,
    113
mineral resources, 88, 95–96, 106

missionaries, 87–88
moraines, 49, 50
mountain glaciers, 40, 49–50
mountains, 47
Murmansk, Russia, 107
musk ox, 55
muskeg, 44
myths and misconceptions, 19–20

N

native peoples
    adaptations of, 7–8, 62–63
    cultural characteristics of, 68–69
    of Eurasia, 74–75
    of ice age, 63–64
    lifestyle changes in, 90–92, 94–95,
        106, 112
    of North America, 69–74
    old world–new world exchanges,
        64–66
    tribal names of, 66–68
natural resources, 14–15, 88, 95–96,
    106, 112
nomadic lifestyle, 68–69, 105
nonnative influences. *See* European
    influences
Nordenskiöld, A. E., 85
Norilsk, Russia, 107
North American peoples, 69–74
North European Plain, 47
North Pole, race to reach, 85
northern lights, 32–33
Northwest Passage, 81–85
Nunavut, Canada, 101

O

ocean currents, and temperature, 22
oil resources, 88, 96, 98
old-world peoples, in settlement of
    Americas, 64–66
organic decay rate, 30–32
otters, sea, 58

P

pack ice, 41
patterned ground, 51

Peary, Robert E., 85
permafrost, 9–10, 34, 42–45
petroleum resources, 88, 96, 98
pingo, 51
plains, 47–48
plant life, 52–54
Pleistocene ice caps, 36–37, 38
polar bear, 57–58
polar hare, 56
polar ice caps, 17, 36–40
Polar World, defined, 8–12
political administration, 90, 97, 113
population, 94, 113
precipitation, 19–20, 26–28
Pytheas of Massilia, 77–78

R

radiation (ground) fog, 29
reindeer, 55, 74–75
reindeer people. *See* Sami
research stations, 90
resources. *See* natural resources
rifle, introduction of, 91–92
river ice, 42
rivers, 60–61
Russia, 90, 106–108. *See also* Siberia
Russian Cossack exploration, 80–81

S

Salekhard, Russia, 107
Sami (Lapps), 67, 68, 74, 106
Samiland (Lappland), 104–106
scientific research, 89–90
sea ice, 40–42
sea level, rise in, 110
sea mammals, 58
sea otters, 58
sea smoke, 30
seals, 58
settlement, 13–14
Seward's Folly, 81
shelf ice, 41
ship navigation, sea ice and, 42
Siberia, 23–24, 28, 47, 48, 106–108
six-month night, 20

snow
   accumulation of, 19–20, 36
   characteristics and prevalence of, 35–36
   uses of, 35–36
   words for, 34
social structure of native cultures, 69
South Pole, 85
strategic importance of Arctic, 88–89, 113
subarctic region. *See* taiga
subpolar region. *See* tundra
suicide rates, 92, 95
summer weather conditions, 24
sunlight duration, and temperature, 20–21
surface color, and temperature, 22

T

taiga, 18–19, 28, 54
telecommunications, 94–95
temperature
   as defining factor of region, 7
   factors controlling, 20–22
   increasing trends in, 42, 45, 110–111
   recorded highs and lows, 23–24
temperature inversions, 25–26
temperature-related phenomena, 24–26
terminal moraines, 49
Thule, 77–78
Titanic, 39–40
traditions of native peoples, 112
Trans-Alaska Pipeline, 96
trapping, 86–87
travel, 35–36, 41–42, 68, 94
treeline, 10
trees, 53, 54
tribal names, 66–68
true north, 10
tundra, 17–18, 27–28, 52–53

V

Vega, 85
Verkhoyansk, Siberia, 23–24, 28

Viking explorations, 78–80
Vineland settlement, 78–79, 80
Vorkuta, Russia, 107

W

walrus, 58
water, bodies of
    lakes and rivers, 59–61
    and temperature, 21–22
water, drinking, scarcity of, 61
waterfowl, 58–59
weather. *See also* temperature
    extreme conditions, 23–24
    fog, 29–30
    myths and misconceptions, 19–20

precipitation, 19–20, 26–28
temperature-related phenomena,
    24–26
wind and windchill, 29, 30–31
Western Siberian Lowland, 47, 48
whales, 58
whaling, 86
white-out conditions, 35
windchill, 30–31
winds, 29
winter weather conditions, 25–26
woodland ecosystem. *See* taiga

Y

Yukon River, 60

About the Author

Charles F. Gritzner is distinguished professor of geography at South Dakota State University in Brookings. He is now in his fifth decade of teaching at the college level, conducting scholarly research, and writing. In addition to teaching, he enjoys traveling, writing, working with teachers, and sharing his love of geography with classroom students and readers alike. As series editor and frequent author for Chelsea House's MODERN WORLD NATIONS and MODERN WORLD CULTURES series, and now author of the three-volume set GEOGRAPHY OF EXTREME ENVIRONMENTS, he has a wonderful opportunity to combine each of these "hobbies."

Professionally, Gritzner has served as both president and executive director of the National Council for Geographic Education. He has received numerous awards in recognition of his academic and teaching achievements, including the NCGE's George J. Miller Award for Distinguished Service to geography and geographic education, the Association of American Geographers Award for Excellence in Teaching, and the Gilbert Grosvenor Honors in Geographic Education.